# Quick and Easy, Proven Recipes

# Soups

**Publisher's Note:** Raw or semi-cooked eggs should not be consumed by babies, toddlers, pregnant or breast-feeding women, the elderly or those suffering from a chronic illness.

**Publisher & Creative Director:** Nick Wells
**Senior Project Editor:** Catherine Taylor
**Art Director:** Mike Spender
**Layout Design:** Jane Ashley
**Digital Design & Production** Chris Herbert

Special thanks to Gina Steer, Robert Zakes and Frances Bodiam.

This is a **FLAME TREE** Book

**FLAME TREE PUBLISHING**
Crabtree Hall, Crabtree Lane
Fulham, London SW6 6TY
United Kingdom
www.flametreepublishing.com

First published 2014

ISBN: 978-1-78361-116-4

Printed in Singapore

Quick and Easy, Proven Recipes

# Soups

**FLAME TREE
PUBLISHING**

# Contents

# Introduction

ℰ

Y̶ou can't beat homemade soups. They can be a light snack or a filling meal; they can be quick and easy with very little preparation or slightly more complicated. Soups are the perfect way to fill up on lots of different healthy vegetables; they are cheap and are always popular. This book will give you plenty of ideas, whether you are making a meal for one or having a formal dinner party.

When preparing soups, there are a few guidelines that will help to make the best soup possible. The quality and condition of the ingredients are very important and they need to be as fresh and in as prime condition as possible, otherwise they may spoil the finished soup. The front section covers all the different herbs and spices you will need in making the perfect soup.

Soups are generally served warm and range from thick and hearty soups, such as Slow-cooked Lamb and Vegetable Soup (*see* page 34) to more delicate creamy soups, including Cream of Mushroom (*see* page 250). They can also be served ice cold, such as Gazpacho (*see* page 194), a perfect way to cool down on a summer's day. Some soups can be served as meals on their own, such as Cock-a-Leekie (*see* page 100) from Scotland. The chicken can be served as a main course and the rest as a soup.

Soups are popular throughout the world and every country and culture has a particular dish. This book covers soups from all corners of the globe – why not try Bulgarian Meatball Soup (*see* page 64) or Thai Spicy Pork Soup (*see* page 38)? Alternatively, try Udon Prawn Noodle Soup (*see* page 134) or classic New England Clam Chowder (*see* page 124), a highly popular soup made from clams and potatoes.

Bread is the traditional accompaniment to most soups, so choose a bread that will suit the flavour and style of the soup. If you are serving a Mexican-style soup, then tortillas are a perfect side dish, whilst flatbreads or chapatis suit a curried soup. You can also serve croutons and toasted bread, such as ciabatta and breadsticks, or if the soup is very filling then just serve it on its own as a meal. Soups suit every occasion and season, so choose a soup and happy cooking.

# Essentials

Great for both lunch and dinner, soups are satisfying and delicious as well as being versatile enough to feature all your favourite ingredients. Before you get stuck in to discovering the range of tempting soups available, take a moment to brush up on your essential knowledge. This chapter guides you through how to enhance your cooking with herbs and spices and how to make sure your soups are meeting your nutritional needs, as well as giving the low-down on food hygiene.

# Herbs ❦ Spices

The use of herbs and spices in home cooking can make all the difference between a bland dish and a tasty one. A variety of the most common herbs and spices, along with their uses, are listed below.

❧ Allspice – The dark allspice berries come whole or ground and have a flavour similar to that of cinnamon, cloves and nutmeg.

❧ Basil – Best fresh, but also available in dried form, basil can be used raw or cooked and works particularly well in tomato-based and Mediterranean dishes.

❧ Bay Leaves – Available in fresh or dried form as well as ground. They make up part of a bouquet garni and are particularly delicious when added to meat and poultry dishes, soups, stews, vegetable dishes and stuffing. They also impart a spicy flavour to milk puddings and egg custards.

❧ Bouquet Garni – A bouquet of fresh herbs tied with a piece of string or in a small piece of muslin. It is used to flavour casseroles, stews and stocks or sauces. The herbs that are normally used are parsley, thyme and bay leaves.

❧ Cayenne – Cayenne is the powdered form of a red chilli pepper said to be native to Cayenne. It is similar in appearance to paprika and can be used sparingly to add a fiery kick to many dishes.

- Cardamom – Cardamom has a distinctive sweet, rich taste and can be bought whole in the pod, in seed form or ground. This sweet, aromatic spice is delicious in curries, rice, and other savoury dishes as well as cakes and biscuits and is great served with rice pudding and fruit.

- Chervil – Reminiscent of parsley and available either in fresh or occasionally dried form, chervil has a faintly sweet, spicy flavour and is particularly good in soups, cheese dishes, stews and with eggs.

- Chilli – Available whole, fresh, dried and in powdered form, red chillies tend to be sweeter in taste than their green counterparts. They are particularly associated with Spanish, Indian and Mexican-style cooking and curries.

- Chives – This member of the onion family is ideal for use when a delicate onion flavour is required. Chives are good with eggs, cheese, fish and vegetable dishes. They also work well as a garnish for soups, meat and vegetable dishes.

- Cloves – Mainly used whole, although available ground, cloves have a very warm, sweet, pungent aroma and can be used to stud roast ham and pork, in mulled wine and punch and when pickling fruit.

- Coriander – Coriander seeds have an orangey flavour and are particularly delicious in casseroles, curries and as a pickling spice. The leaves and roots, which are thoroughly washed first, are used both to flavour spicy, aromatic dishes and as a garnish.

- Cumin – Available ground or as whole seeds, cumin has a strong, slightly bitter flavour. It is one of the main ingredients in curry powder and complements many fish, meat and rice dishes.

Herbs & Spices

❧ Ginger – Ginger comes in many forms, but primarily as a fresh root and in dried ground form, which can be used in baking, curries, pickles, sauces and Chinese cooking.

❧ Lemongrass – Available fresh and dried, with a subtle, aromatic, lemony flavour, lemongrass is essential to Thai cooking. It is also delicious when added to soups, poultry and fish dishes.

❧ Marjoram – Often dried, marjoram has a sweet, slightly spicy flavour, which tastes fantastic when added to stuffing, meat or tomato-based dishes.

❧ Oregano – The strongly flavoured dried leaves are similar to marjoram and are used extensively in Italian and Greek cooking.

❧ Paprika – Paprika often comes in two varieties. One is quite sweet and mild and the other has a slight bite to it. Paprika is made from the fruit of the sweet pepper and is good in meat and poultry dishes and as a garnish. The rule of buying herbs and spices little and often applies particularly to paprika, as unfortunately it does not keep especially well.

❧ Parsley – The stems as well as the leaves of parsley can be used to complement most savoury dishes, as they contain the most flavour. They can also be used as a garnish.

❧ Pepper – This comes as white and black peppercorns and is best freshly ground. Both add flavour to most dishes, sauces and gravies. Black pepper has a more robust flavour, while white pepper has a much more delicate flavour.

**Rosemary** – The small, needle-like leaves have a sweet aroma which is particularly good with lamb, stuffing and vegetable dishes.

**Saffron** – Deep orange in colour, saffron is traditionally used in paella, rice and cakes, but is also delicious with poultry. Reputed to be worth more than gold, saffron is highly prized.

**Sage** – The fresh or dried leaves have a pungent, slightly bitter taste, which is delicious with pork and poultry, sausages, stuffing and as a simple accompaniment to stuffed pasta when tossed in a little butter.

**Savory** – This herb resembles thyme, but has a softer flavour that particularly complements all types of fish and beans.

**Tarragon** – A popular herb in French cuisine, the fresh or dried leaves of tarragon have a sweet, aromatic taste, which is particularly good with poultry, seafood and fish.

**Thyme** – Available fresh or dried, thyme has a pungent flavour and is included in bouquet garni. It complements many meat and poultry dishes and stuffing.

**Turmeric** – This root is ground and has a brilliant yellow colour. It has a bitter, peppery flavour and is often used in curry powder and mustard spice mixes.

# Nutrition

*Home-cooked meals are a great way to provide us with a healthy and well-balanced diet, the body's primary energy source. In children, a healthy diet is the basis of future health and provides lots of energy. In adults, it encourages self-healing and regeneration within the body. A well-balanced, varied diet will provide the body with all the essential nutrients it needs. The ideal variety of foods is shown in the pyramid below.

## Fats

Fats fall into two categories: saturated and unsaturated fats. It is very important that a healthy balance is achieved within the diet. Fats are an essential part of the diet and a source of energy and provide essential fatty acids and fat–soluble vitamins. The right balance of fats should boost the body's immunity to infection and keep muscles, nerves and arteries in good condition. Saturated fats are of animal origin and are hard when stored at room temperature. They can be found in dairy produce, meat, eggs, margarines and hard, white cooking fat (lard) as well as in manufactured products such as pies, biscuits and cakes. A high intake of saturated fat over many years has been proven to increase heart disease and high blood cholesterol levels and often leads to weight gain. The aim of a healthy diet is to keep the fat content low in the foods that we eat. Lowering the amount of saturated fat that we consume is very important, but this does not mean that it is good to consume lots of other types of fat.

*Fats*

milk, yogurt
and cheese

*Proteins*

meat, fish, poultry, eggs,
nuts and pulses

*Fruits and
Vegetables*

*Starchy Carbohydrates*

cereals, potatoes, bread, rice and pasta

There are two kinds of unsaturated fats: polyunsaturated fats and monounsaturated fats. Polyunsaturated fats include the following oils: safflower oil, soybean oil, corn oil and sesame oil. Within the polyunsaturated group are Omega oils. The Omega-3 oils are of significant interest because they have been found to be particularly beneficial to coronary health and can encourage brain growth and development. Omega-3 oils are derived from oily fish such as salmon, mackerel, herring, pilchards and sardines. It is recommended that we should eat these types of fish at least once a week. However, for those who do not eat fish or who are vegetarians, flaxseed oil supplements are available in most supermarkets and health shops. It is suggested that these supplements should be taken on a daily basis. The most popular oils that are high in monounsaturates are olive oil, sunflower oil and peanut oil. The Mediterranean diet, which is based on foods high in monounsaturated fats, is recommended for heart health. Also, monounsaturated fats are known to help reduce the levels of LDL (the bad) cholesterol.

## Proteins

Composed of amino acids (proteins' building bricks), proteins perform a wide variety of functions for the body, including supplying energy and building and repairing tissue. Good sources of proteins are eggs, milk, yogurt, cheese, meat, fish, poultry, nuts and pulses. (*See* the second level of the pyramid.) Some of these foods, however, contain saturated fats. For a nutritional balance, eat generous amounts of soya beans, lentils, peas and nuts.

## Fruits and Vegetables

Not only are fruits and vegetables the most visually appealing foods, but they are extremely good for us, providing vital vitamins and minerals essential for growth, repair and protection in the human body. Fruits and vegetables are low in

Nutrition

calories and are responsible for regulating the body's metabolic processes and controlling the composition of its fluids and cells.

# Minerals

∾ Calcium – Important for healthy bones and teeth, nerve transmission, muscle contraction, blood clotting and hormone function. Calcium promotes a healthy heart, improves skin, relieves aching muscles and bones, maintains the correct acid-alkaline balance and reduces menstrual cramps. Good sources are dairy products, small bones of small fish, nuts, pulses, fortified white flours, breads and green, leafy vegetables.

∾ Chromium – Part of the glucose tolerance factor, chromium balances blood sugar levels, helps to normalise hunger and reduce cravings, improves lifespan, helps protect DNA and is essential for heart function. Good sources are brewer's yeast, wholemeal bread, rye bread, oysters, potatoes, green peppers, butter and parsnips.

∾ Iodine – Important for thyroid hormones and for normal development. Good sources of iodine are seafood, seaweed, milk and dairy products.

∾ Iron – As a component of haemoglobin, iron carries oxygen around the body. It is vital for normal growth and development. Good sources are liver, corned beef, red meat, fortified breakfast cereals, pulses, green, leafy vegetables, egg yolk and cocoa and cocoa products.

∾ Magnesium – Important for efficient functioning of metabolic enzymes and development of the skeleton. Magnesium promotes healthy muscles by helping them to relax and is therefore good for PMS. It is also important for heart muscles and the nervous system. Good sources are nuts, green vegetables, meat, cereals, milk and yogurt.

ॐ **Phosphorus** – Forms and maintains bones and teeth, builds muscle tissue, helps maintain the body's pH and aids metabolism and energy production. Phosphorus is present in almost all foods.

ॐ **Potassium** – Enables nutrients to move into cells, while waste products move out; promotes healthy nerves and muscles; maintains fluid balance in the body; helps secretion of insulin for blood sugar control to produce constant energy; relaxes muscles; maintains heart functioning and stimulates gut movement to encourage proper elimination. Good sources are fruit, vegetables, milk and bread.

ॐ **Selenium** – Antioxidant properties help to protect against free radicals and carcinogens. Selenium reduces inflammation, stimulates the immune system to fight infections, promotes a healthy heart and helps vitamin E's action. It is also required for the male reproductive system and is needed for metabolism. Good sources are tuna, liver, kidney, meat, eggs, cereals, nuts and dairy products.

ॐ **Sodium** – Helps to control body fluid and balance, preventing dehydration. Sodium is involved in muscle and nerve function and helps move nutrients into cells. All foods are good sources, but pickled and salted foods are richest in sodium.

ॐ **Zinc** – Important for metabolism and the healing of wounds. It also aids ability to cope with stress, promotes a healthy nervous system and brain, especially in the growing foetus, aids bone and tooth formation and is essential for constant energy. Good sources are liver, meat, pulses, wholegrain cereals, nuts and oysters.

# Vitamins

- **Vitamin A** – Important for cell growth and development and for the formation of visual pigments in the eye. Found in liver, meat, whole milk, red and yellow fruits and carrots.

- **Vitamin B1** – Important in releasing energy from carbohydrate-containing foods. Good sources are yeast and yeast products, bread, fortified breakfast cereals and potatoes.

- **Vitamin B2** – Important for metabolism of proteins, fats and carbohydrates. Found in meat, yeast extract, fortified cereals and milk.

- **Vitamin B3** – Helps the metabolism of food into energy. Sources are milk and milk products, fortified breakfast cereals, pulses, meat, poultry and eggs.

- **Vitamin B5** – Important for the metabolism of food and energy production. All foods are good sources, but especially fortified breakfast cereals, wholegrain bread and dairy products.

- **Vitamin B6** – Important for metabolism of protein and fat. Vitamin B6 may also be involved with the regulation of sex hormones. Good sources are liver, fish, pork, soya beans and peanuts.

- **Vitamin B12** – Important for the production of red blood cells and DNA. It is vital for growth and the nervous system. Good sources are meat, fish, eggs, poultry and milk.

- **Biotin** – Important for metabolism of fatty acids. Good sources of biotin are liver, kidney, eggs and nuts. Micro-organisms also manufacture this vitamin in the gut.

- ∾ Vitamin C – Important for healing wounds and the formation of collagen, which keeps skin and bones strong. It is an important antioxidant. Sources are fruits and vegetables.

- ∾ Vitamin D – Important for absorption of calcium to build bone strength. Sources are oily fish, eggs, whole milk and milk products, margarine and sunlight – vitamin D is made in the skin.

- ∾ Vitamin E – Important as an antioxidant vitamin, helping to protect cell membranes from damage. Good sources are vegetable oils, margarines, seeds, nuts and green vegetables.

- ∾ Folic Acid – Critical during pregnancy for the development of foetus brain and nerves. It is essential for brain and nerve function and is needed for protein and red blood cell formation. Sources are wholegrain cereals, fortified cereals, green, leafy vegetables, oranges and liver.

- ∾ Vitamin K – Important for controlling blood clotting. Sources are cauliflower, Brussels sprouts, lettuce, cabbage, beans, broccoli, peas, asparagus, potatoes, corn oil, tomatoes and milk.

# Carbohydrates

Carbohydrates come in two basic forms: starchy and sugar carbohydrates. Starchy carbohydrates, also known as complex carbohydrates, include cereals, potatoes, breads, rice and pasta. (*See* the fourth level of the pyramid). Eating wholegrain varieties also provides fibre, beneficial in preventing bowel cancer, and controlling cholesterol levels. Sugar carbohydrates, known as fast-release carbohydrates (because of the quick fix of energy they give), include sugar and sugar-sweetened products such as jams and syrups. Milk provides lactose, which is milk sugar, and fruits provide fructose, which is fruit sugar.

# Hygiene in the Kitchen

I t is well worth remembering that many foods can carry some form of bacteria. In most cases, the worst it will lead to is a bout of food poisoning or gastroenteritis, although for certain people this can be more serious. The risk can be reduced or eliminated by good food hygiene and proper cooking.

Do not buy food that is past its sell-by date and do not consume any food that is past its use-by date. When buying food, use your eyes and nose. If the food looks tired, limp or a bad colour or it has a rank, acrid or simply bad smell, do not buy or eat it under any circumstances. Do take special care when preparing raw meat and fish.

A separate chopping board should be used for each food; wash the knife, board and the hands thoroughly before handling or preparing any other food.

Regularly clean, defrost and clear out the refrigerator or freezer – it is worth checking the packaging to see exactly how long each product is safe to freeze.

Avoid handling food if suffering from an upset stomach, as bacteria can be passed on through food preparation.

Dish cloths and tea towels must be washed and changed regularly. Ideally, use disposable cloths, which should be replaced on a daily basis. More durable cloths should be left to soak in bleach, then washed in the washing machine on a boil wash.

Keep hands, cooking utensils and food preparation surfaces clean and do not allow pets to climb onto any work surfaces.

## Buying

Avoid bulk buying where possible, especially fresh produce such as meat, poultry, fish, fruit and vegetables, unless buying for the freezer. Fresh foods lose their nutritional value rapidly, so buying a little at a time minimises loss of nutrients. It also eliminates a packed refrigerator, which reduces the effectiveness of the refrigeration process.

When buying prepackaged goods such as cans or pots of cream and yogurts, check that the packaging is intact and not damaged or pierced at all. Cans should not be dented, pierced or rusty. Check the sell-by dates even for cans and packets of dry ingredients such as flour and rice. Store fresh foods in the refrigerator as soon as possible – not in the car or the office.

When buying frozen foods, ensure that they are not heavily iced on the outside and the contents feel completely frozen. Ensure that the frozen foods have been stored in the cabinet at the correct storage level and the temperature is below -18°C/-0.4°F. Pack in cool bags to transport home and place in the freezer as soon as possible after purchase.

## Preparation

Make sure that all work surfaces and utensils are clean and dry. Hygiene should be given priority at all times. Separate chopping boards should be used for raw and cooked meats, fish and vegetables. Currently, a variety of good-quality plastic boards come in various designs and colours. This makes differentiating easier and the plastic has the added hygienic

advantage of being washable at high temperatures in the dishwasher. (NB: If using the board for fish, first wash in cold water, then in hot, to prevent odour!) Also, remember that knives and utensils should always be thoroughly cleaned after use.

When cooking, be particularly careful to keep cooked and raw food separate to avoid any contamination. It is worth washing all fruits and vegetables, regardless of whether they are going to be eaten raw or lightly cooked. This rule should apply even to prewashed herbs and salads.

Do not reheat food more than once. If using a microwave, always check that the food is piping hot all the way through. In theory, the food should reach a minimum temperature of 70°C/158°F and needs to be cooked at that temperature for at least 3 minutes to ensure that any bacteria in the food are killed.

All poultry must be thoroughly thawed before using, including chicken and poussin. Remove the food to be thawed from the freezer and place in a shallow dish to contain the juices.

Leave the food in the refrigerator until it is completely thawed. A 1.4 kg/3 lb whole chicken will take about 26–30 hours to thaw. To speed up the process, immerse the chicken in cold water. However, make sure that the water is changed regularly. When the joints can move freely and no ice crystals remain in the cavity, the bird is completely thawed.

Once thawed, remove the wrapper and pat the chicken dry. Place the chicken in a shallow dish, cover lightly and, if storing, store as close to the base of the refrigerator as possible. The chicken should be cooked as soon as possible.

Some foods can be cooked from frozen, including many prepacked foods such as soups, sauces, casseroles and breads. Where applicable, follow the manufacturers' instructions.

Vegetables and fruits can also be cooked from frozen, but meats and fish should be thawed first. The only time food can be refrozen is when the food has been thoroughly thawed, then cooked. Once the food has cooled, then it can be frozen again. On such occasions, the food can only be stored for one month.

All poultry and game (except for duck) must be cooked thoroughly. When cooked, the juices will run clear from the thickest part of the bird – the best area to try is usually the thigh. Other meats, such as minced meat and pork, should be cooked right the way through. Fish should turn opaque, be firm in texture and break easily into large flakes.

When cooking leftovers, make sure they are reheated until piping hot and that any sauce or soup reaches boiling point first before eating.

## Storing, Refrigerating and Freezing

Meat, poultry, fish, seafood and dairy products should all be refrigerated. The temperature of the refrigerator should be between 1–5°C/34–41°F, while the freezer temperature should not rise above -18°C/-0.4°F.

To ensure the optimum refrigerator and freezer temperature, avoid leaving the door open for a long time. Try not to overstock the refrigerator, as this reduces the airflow inside and affects the

efficiency in cooling the food within. When refrigerating cooked food, allow it to cool down quickly and completely before refrigerating. Hot food will raise the temperature of the refrigerator and possibly affect or spoil other food stored in it.

Food within the refrigerator and freezer should always be covered. Raw and cooked food should be stored in separate parts of the refrigerator. Cooked food should be kept on the top shelves of the refrigerator, while raw meat, poultry and fish should be placed on bottom shelves to avoid drips and cross-contamination.

It is recommended that eggs should be refrigerated in order to maintain their freshness and shelf life.

Take care that frozen foods are not stored in the freezer for too long. Blanched vegetables can be stored for one month; beef, lamb, poultry and pork for six months; and unblanched vegetables and fruits in syrup for a year. Oily fish and sausages can be stored for three months. Dairy products can last four to six months, while cakes and pastries can be kept in the freezer for three to six months.

## High-risk Foods

Certain foods may carry risks to people who are considered vulnerable, such as the elderly, the ill, pregnant or breast-feeding women, babies, young infants and those suffering from a recurring illness. It is advisable to avoid those foods listed below, which belong to a higher-risk category.

There is a slight chance that some eggs carry the bacteria salmonella. Cook eggs until both the yolk and the white are firm to eliminate this risk.

Pay particular attention to dishes and products incorporating lightly cooked or raw eggs, which should be eliminated from the diet. Sauces including Hollandaise, mayonnaise, mousses, soufflés and meringues all use raw or lightly cooked eggs, as do custard-based dishes, ice creams and sorbets. These are all considered high-risk foods to the vulnerable groups mentioned above.

Certain meats and poultry also carry the potential risk of salmonella and so should be cooked thoroughly until the juices run clear and there is no pinkness left. Unpasteurised products such as milk, cheese (especially soft cheese), pâté and meat (both raw and cooked) all have the potential risk of listeria and should be avoided.

When buying seafood, buy from a reputable source which has a high turnover to ensure freshness. Fish should have bright, clear eyes, shiny skin and bright pink or red gills. The fish should feel stiff to the touch, with a slight smell of sea air and iodine. The flesh of fish steaks and fillets should be translucent, with no signs of discolouration.

Molluscs such as scallops, clams and mussels are sold fresh and are still alive. Avoid any that are open or do not close when tapped lightly. In the same way, univalves such as whelks or winkles should withdraw back into their shells when lightly prodded. When choosing cephalopods such as squid and octopus, they should have a firm flesh and pleasant sea smell.

As with all fish, whether it is shellfish or wet fish, care is required when freezing it. It is imperative to check whether the fish has been frozen before. If it has been frozen, then it should not be frozen again under any circumstances.

Hygiene in the Kitchen

Meat

With its intense savoury flavour and rich aromas, meat is an excellent base for many soups. Whether you are after a light and brothy soup or a more hearty and filling option, there is a soup for every meat lover. If you're looking for something a little different, try the delicately spiced Miso Ramen Soup or the tasty Bulgarian Meatball Soup. For those with a more traditional taste, the Winter Hotchpot is the perfect hearty lunch choice for a chilly day.

# Classic Minestrone

## Serves 6–8

25 g/1 oz butter
3 tbsp olive oil
3 rashers streaky bacon
1 large onion, peeled
1 garlic clove, peeled
1 celery stalk, trimmed
2 carrots, peeled
400 g can chopped tomatoes
1.1 litres/2 pints chicken stock
175 g/6 oz green cabbage,
finely shredded
50 g/2 oz French beans, trimmed
and halved
3 tbsp frozen petits pois
50 g/2 oz spaghetti, broken into
short pieces
salt and freshly ground
black pepper
Parmesan cheese shavings,
to garnish
crusty bread, to serve

Heat the butter and olive oil together in a large saucepan. Chop the bacon and add to the saucepan. Cook for 3–4 minutes, then remove with a slotted spoon and reserve.

Finely chop the onion, garlic, celery and carrots and add to the saucepan, one ingredient at a time, stirring well after each addition. Cover and cook gently for 8–10 minutes until the vegetables are softened.

Add the chopped tomatoes with their juice and the stock, bring to the boil, then cover the saucepan with a lid, reduce the heat and simmer gently for about 20 minutes.

Stir in the cabbage, beans, peas and spaghetti pieces. Cover and simmer for a further 20 minutes, or until all the ingredients are tender. Season to taste with salt and pepper.

Return the cooked bacon to the saucepan and bring the soup to the boil. Serve the soup immediately with Parmesan cheese shavings sprinkled on the top and plenty of crusty bread to accompany it.

# Kharcho (Georgian Meat Soup)

## Serves 4

1 tbsp sunflower oil
900 g/2 lb neck of lamb, cut into
individual pieces
1 onion, peeled and chopped
2 garlic cloves, peeled and chopped
1.7 litres/3 pints water
¹/₂ tsp paprika
¹/₂ tsp dried thyme
¹/₂ tsp salt
1 tsp freshly chopped coriander
2 celery stalks, trimmed
and chopped
1 carrot, peeled and chopped
freshly ground black pepper
few dashes hot chilli sauce,
or to taste
1 tsp soft brown sugar
2 tbsp tomato purée
2 tbsp freshly squeezed lemon juice
3 garlic cloves, peeled and crushed
150 ml/¹/₄ pint red wine
rye or sourdough bread, to serve

Heat the oil in a frying pan, add the lamb and fry on all sides until browned. Remove and place in a large saucepan. Add the onion and garlic to the frying pan and cook for 5 minutes, or until the onion is beginning to soften, then remove and add to the lamb. Pour in the water.

Add all the dried herbs to the saucepan with the salt, then bring to the boil. Reduce the heat to a simmer, cover with a lid and cook for 30 minutes.

After 30 minutes, add all the remaining ingredients including the wine and cook for a further 15 minutes. Adjust the seasoning and cook for a further 20 minutes, or until all the meat is tender. Serve with bread.

**Cook's Tip:** This soup can be made with either beef, pork, lamb or chicken.

# Wonton Noodle Soup

## Serves 4

4 shiitake mushrooms, wiped
125 g/4 oz raw prawns, peeled
and finely chopped
125 g/4 oz pork mince
4 water chestnuts, finely chopped
4 spring onions, trimmed and
finely sliced
1 medium egg white
salt and freshly ground
black pepper
1½ tsp cornflour
1 packet fresh wonton wrappers
1.1 litres/2 pints chicken stock
2 cm/¾ inch piece root ginger,
peeled and sliced
75 g/3 oz thin egg noodles
125 g/4 oz pak choi, shredded

Place the mushrooms in a bowl, cover with warm water and leave to soak for 1 hour. Drain, remove and discard the stalks and finely chop the mushrooms. Return to the bowl with the prawns, pork, water chestnuts, 2 of the spring onions and egg white. Season to taste with salt and pepper. Mix well.

Mix the cornflour with 1 tablespoon cold water to make a paste. Place a wonton wrapper on a board and brush the edges with the paste. Drop a little less than 1 teaspoon of the pork mixture in the centre, then fold in half to make a triangle, pressing the edges together. Bring the two outer corners together, fixing together with a little more paste. Continue until all the pork mixture is used up; you should have 16–20 wontons.

Pour the stock into a large, wide saucepan, add the ginger slices and bring to the boil. Add the wontons and simmer for about 5 minutes. Add the noodles and cook for 1 minute. Stir in the pak choi and cook for a further 2 minutes, or until the noodles and pak choi are tender and the wontons have floated to the surface and are cooked through.

Ladle the soup into warmed bowls, discarding the ginger. Sprinkle with the remaining sliced spring onions and serve immediately.

# Slow-cooked Lamb & Vegetable Soup

## Serves 4

pinch saffron strands
4 tbsp warm water
2 tbsp olive oil
350 g/12 oz lamb fillet, trimmed of
fat and cut into chunks
2–3 garlic cloves, peeled
and chopped
2 medium onions, peeled
and chopped
300 g/11 oz carrots, peeled
and chopped
350 g/12 oz potatoes, peeled
and chopped
2 parsnips, peeled and chopped
400 g can chopped tomatoes
900 ml/1½ pints vegetable stock
salt and freshly ground
black pepper
1 small rosemary sprig
2 medium tomatoes, cut into
small pieces
flat-leaf parsley and thyme
sprigs, to garnish

Place the saffron in a small bowl and pour over the warm water. Leave for 15 minutes.

Heat the oil in a large frying pan, add the lamb and fry until browned. Add the garlic and onions and fry for a further 10 minutes. Add the carrots, potatoes and parsnips and fry for a further 5 minutes. Place in a large saucepan.

Add the canned tomatoes together with the saffron and its soaking liquid and the stock. Season to taste and add the rosemary. Bring to the boil, then reduce the heat to a simmer. Add the fresh tomatoes.

Simmer very gently for 1½–2 hours until the lamb and vegetables are tender. Serve in warmed bowls garnished with fresh parsley and thyme.

# Chinese Leaf & Mushroom Soup

## Serves 4–6

450 g/1 lb Chinese leaves
25 g/1 oz dried Chinese (shiitake) mushrooms
1 tbsp vegetable oil
75 g/3 oz smoked streaky bacon, diced
2.5 cm/1 inch piece fresh root ginger, peeled and finely chopped
175 g/6 oz chestnut mushrooms, thinly sliced
1.1 litres/2 pints chicken stock
4–6 spring onions, trimmed and cut into short lengths
2 tbsp dry sherry or Chinese rice wine
salt and freshly ground black pepper
sesame oil, for drizzling

Trim the stem ends of the Chinese leaves and cut in half lengthways. Remove the triangular core with a knife, then cut into 2.5 cm/1 inch slices and reserve. Place the dried Chinese mushrooms in a bowl and pour over enough almost-boiling water to cover. Leave to stand for 20 minutes to soften, then gently lift out and squeeze out the liquid. Discard the stems and thinly slice the caps and reserve. Strain the liquid through a muslin-lined sieve or a coffee filter paper and reserve.

Heat a wok over a medium-high heat, add the oil and, when hot, add the bacon. Stir-fry for 3–4 minutes until crisp and golden, stirring frequently. Add the ginger and chestnut mushrooms and stir-fry for a further 2–3 minutes.

Add the chicken stock and bring to the boil, skimming any fat and scum that rises to the surface. Add the spring onions, sherry or rice wine, Chinese leaves and sliced Chinese mushrooms and season to taste with salt and pepper. Pour in the reserved soaking liquid and reduce the heat to the lowest possible setting.

Simmer gently, covered, until all the vegetables are very tender; this will take about 10 minutes. Add a little water if the liquid has reduced too much. Spoon into soup bowls and drizzle with a little sesame oil. Serve immediately.

# Thai Spicy Pork Soup

## Serves 4

1 tbsp vegetable oil
225 g/8 oz pork fillet, trimmed and cut into small pieces
1.1 litres/2 pints pork or chicken stock
1 red chilli, deseeded and finely chopped
1 lemongrass stalk, trimmed and sliced
6 shiitake mushrooms
$^1/_2$ tsp soy sauce, or to taste
$^1/_2$ tsp oyster sauce, or to taste
$^1/_2$ tsp caster sugar
2 garlic cloves, peeled and thinly sliced
75 g/3 oz canned water chestnuts
3–4 spring onions, trimmed and sliced diagonally into 5 cm/ 2 inch pieces
75 g/3 oz pak choi, trimmed

## To garnish:

Thai basil
pinch dried chill flakes (optional)

Heat the oil in a frying pan, add the pork and fry until browned on both sides. Remove and drain on kitchen paper. Reserve both the pork and oil.

Place the stock in a large saucepan together with the chopped chilli, lemongrass, mushrooms, soy sauce, oyster sauce and sugar. Bring to the boil then reduce the heat and simmer for 15 minutes.

Reheat the reserved oil in a frying pan, add the garlic and fry for 1 minute. Remove the garlic from the oil, discarding the oil. Add the garlic to the stock together with the reserved pork and water chestnuts and cook for a further 15 minutes before adding the spring onions and pak choi. Serve in warm bowls garnished with Thai basil and dried chill flakes, if liked.

**Cook's Tip:** both soy and oyster sauces are strong in flavour so use sparingly to begin with, say $^1/_2$ teaspoon then increase if liked.

# Vietnamese Beef & Rice Noodle Soup

## Serves 4–6

### For the beef stock:

900 g/2 lb meaty beef bones
1 large onion, peeled and quartered
2 carrots, peeled and cut into chunks
2 celery stalks, trimmed and sliced
1 leek, washed and sliced
into chunks
2 garlic cloves, unpeeled and
lightly crushed
3 whole star anise
1 tsp black peppercorns

### For the soup:

175 g/6 oz dried rice stick noodles
4–6 spring onions, trimmed and
diagonally sliced
1 red chilli, deseeded and
diagonally sliced
1 small bunch fresh coriander
1 small bunch fresh mint
350 g/12 oz fillet steak, very
thinly sliced
salt and freshly ground black pepper

Place all the ingredients for the beef stock into a large stock pot or saucepan and cover with cold water. Bring to the boil and skim off any scum that rises to the surface. Reduce the heat and simmer gently, partially covered, for 2–3 hours, skimming occasionally.

Strain into a large bowl and leave to cool, then skim off the fat. Chill in the refrigerator and, when cold, remove any fat from the surface. Pour 1.7 litres/3 pints of the stock into a large wok and reserve.

Cover the noodles with warm water and leave for 3 minutes, or until just softened. Drain, then cut into 10 cm/4 inch lengths.

Arrange the spring onions and chilli on a serving platter or large plate. Strip the leaves from the coriander and mint and arrange them in piles on the plate.

Bring the stock in the wok to the boil over a high heat. Add the noodles and simmer for about 2 minutes until tender. Add the beef strips and simmer for about 1 minute. Season to taste with salt and pepper.

Ladle the soup with the noodles and beef strips into individual soup bowls and serve immediately, with the plate of condiments handed around separately.

# Solyanka (Sour & Spicy Russian Soup)

### Serves 4

### For the bouquet garni:
2 fresh bay leaves
6 black peppercorns
3 whole cloves
1 cinnamon stick

### For the soup:
1.1 litres/2 pints water
1 small cabbage, outer leaves and
hard core discarded
2 celery stalks, trimmed and chopped
1 tbsp vegetable oil
1 onion, peeled and chopped
1 large carrot, peeled and chopped
225 g/8 oz Polish beef sausage,
cut into chunks
225 g/8 oz ham in one piece, cubed
2 skinless chicken leg joints, halved
1 tbsp tomato purée
1 large dill pickled cucumber,
sliced or chopped
1 lemon, thinly sliced into half moons
50 g/2 oz green and black olives,
pitted and cut in half

Tie all the ingredients for the bouquet garni in a piece of muslin and place in a large saucepan. Add the water and bring to the boil. Reduce the heat, add the cabbage and celery and simmer for 30 minutes.

Heat the oil in another saucepan, add the onion, carrot, sausage, ham and chicken and cook for 5–8 minutes until the onion is beginning to soften.

Blend the tomato purée with the stock, then pour into the pan, then add the pickled cucumber and lemon and bring to the boil. Reduce the heat and simmer for 10 minutes. Add the olives and continue to cook until piping hot. Serve.

# Cawl

700 g/1¹/₂ lb scrag end of lamb or
best end of neck chops
pinch salt
2 large onions, peeled and
thinly sliced
3 large potatoes, peeled and cut
into chunks
2 parsnips, peeled and cut
into chunks
1 swede, peeled and cut
into chunks
3 large carrots, peeled and cut
into chunks
2 leeks, trimmed and sliced
freshly ground black pepper
4 tbsp freshly chopped parsley
warm crusty bread, to serve

Put the lamb in a large saucepan, cover with cold water and bring to the boil. Add a generous pinch of salt. Simmer gently for 1¹/₂ hours, then set aside to cool completely, preferably overnight.

The next day, skim the fat off the surface of the lamb liquid and discard. Return the saucepan to the heat and bring back to the boil. Simmer for 5 minutes. Add the onions, potatoes, parsnips, swede and carrots and return to the boil. Reduce the heat, cover and cook for about 20 minutes, stirring occasionally.

Add the leeks and season to taste with salt and pepper. Cook for a further 10 minutes, or until all the vegetables are tender.

Using a slotted spoon, remove the meat from the saucepan and take the meat off the bone. Discard the bones and any gristle, then return the meat to the pan. Adjust the seasoning to taste, stir in the parsley, then serve immediately with plenty of warm crusty bread.

# Miso Ramen Soup

## Serves 4

1 tsp vegetable oil
1 garlic clove, peeled and crushed
1–2 tsp freshly grated root ginger
4 shiitake mushrooms, sliced
1 medium carrot, peeled and cut
into matchsticks
900 ml/1½ pints vegetable stock
1 tsp soft brown sugar
2 tsp soy sauce, or to taste
2 tbsp miso paste
125 g/4 oz beansprouts
225 g/8 oz ramen noodles, cooked
according to the packet instructions
1 tsp sesame oil
4 hard-boiled eggs
6–8 parsley sprigs
350 g/12 oz thickly cut ham,
cut in half

Heat a wok for 30 seconds, then add the oil. Swirl until the wok is lightly coated in the oil, then add the garlic, ginger and shiitake mushrooms and stir-fry for 1 minute.

Add the carrots to the wok together with the stock. Add the sugar and soy sauce and bring to the boil. Cook for 2 minutes.

Reduce the heat to a simmer and add the miso paste. Slowly stir until the miso paste is completely dissolved. Add the beansprouts and the noodles.

Ladle into soup bowls. Drizzle over the sesame oil and place 2 halves of hard-boiled egg, some fresh parsley and the ham on top and serve.

**Cook's Tip:** Miso paste is used in Japanese cooking and is made from fermented soya beans.

# Beef Noodle Soup

## Serves 4

900 g/2 lb boneless shin or
braising steak
1 cinnamon stick
2 star anise
2 tbsp light soy sauce
6 dried red chillies or 3 fresh,
chopped in half
2 dried citrus peels, soaked and
diced (optional)
1.1 litres/2 pints beef or
chicken stock
350 g/12 oz egg noodles
2 spring onions, trimmed and
chopped, to garnish
warm chunks crusty farmhouse
bread, to serve (optional)

Trim the meat of any fat and sinew, then cut into thin strips. Place the meat, cinnamon, star anise, soy sauce, red chillies, chopped citrus peels (if using) and stock into the wok. Bring to the boil, then reduce the heat to a simmer. Skim off any fat or scum that floats to the surface. Cover the wok and simmer for about 1$^1$/$_2$ hours until the meat is tender.

Meanwhile, bring a saucepan of lightly salted water to the boil, then add the noodles and cook in the boiling water for 3–4 minutes until tender or according to packet instructions. Drain well and reserve.

When the meat is tender, add the noodles to the wok and simmer for a further 1–2 minutes until the noodles are heated through thoroughly. Ladle the soup into warmed shallow soup bowls or dishes and scatter with chopped spring onions. Serve, if liked, with chunks of warm crusty bread.

# White Bean Soup with Parmesan Croutons

⁊

## Serves 4

3 thick slices white bread, cut into 1 cm/$\frac{1}{2}$ inch cubes
3 tbsp groundnut oil
2 tbsp Parmesan cheese, finely grated
1 tbsp light olive oil
1 large onion, peeled and finely chopped
50 g/2 oz unsmoked bacon lardons (or thick slices bacon, diced)
1 tbsp fresh thyme leaves
2 x 400 g can cannellini beans, drained
900 ml/1$\frac{1}{2}$ pints chicken stock
salt and freshly ground black pepper
1 tbsp prepared pesto sauce
50 g/2 oz piece pepperoni sausage, diced
1 tbsp fresh lemon juice
1 tbsp fresh basil, roughly shredded

Preheat the oven to 200°C/400°F/Gas Mark 6. Place the cubes of bread in a bowl and pour over the groundnut oil. Stir to coat the bread, then sprinkle over the Parmesan cheese. Place on a lightly oiled baking tray and bake in the preheated oven for 10 minutes, or until crisp and golden.

Heat the olive oil in a large saucepan and cook the onion for 4–5 minutes until softened. Add the bacon and thyme and cook for a further 3 minutes. Stir in the beans, stock and black pepper and simmer gently for 5 minutes.

Place half the bean mixture and liquid into a food processor and blend until smooth.

Return the purée to the saucepan. Stir in the pesto sauce, pepperoni sausage and lemon juice and season to taste with salt and pepper.

Return the soup to the heat and cook for a further 2–3 minutes until piping hot. Place some of the beans in each serving bowl and add a ladleful of soup. Garnish with shredded basil and serve immediately with the croutons scattered over the top.

# Yukgaejang (Korean Spiced Beef Soup)

## Serves 4

350 g/12 oz beef, such as brisket
1.1 litres/2 pints water
2 garlic cloves, peeled
and crushed
8 spring onions, trimmed
and shredded
125 g/4 oz fine French beans,
trimmed and diagonally sliced
125 g/4 oz beansprouts
salt and freshly ground
black pepper
1 tsp hot chilli sauce
2 tsp soy sauce
225 g/8 oz cooked egg or
glass noodles
1 medium egg, beaten
1 tsp sesame oil

Place the beef in a large saucepan with the water and bring to the boil. Reduce the heat, cover with a lid and simmer for at least 1 hour until tender, skimming off any scum that rises to the top.

Remove the beef and leave to cool, leaving the broth in the pan. Sprinkle the garlic over the cooled meat, then shred finely and place in a bowl. Add the spring onions, the beans and beansprouts and stir lightly until combined. Season with salt, pepper and the hot chilli and soy sauces.

Return the beef mixture to the stock in the saucepan together with the noodles and bring to the boil. Reduce the heat and simmer for 5 minutes before swirling in the beaten egg and sesame oil and serving.

# Bacon ❧ Split Pea Soup

## Serves 4

50 g/2 oz dried split peas
25 g/1 oz butter
1 garlic clove, peeled and
finely chopped
1 medium onion, peeled and
thinly sliced
175 g/6 oz long-grain rice
2 tbsp tomato purée
1.1 litres/2 pints vegetable or
chicken stock
175 g/6 oz carrots, peeled and
finely diced
125 g/4 oz streaky bacon,
finely chopped
salt and freshly ground
black pepper
2 tbsp freshly chopped parsley
4 tbsp single cream
warm crusty garlic bread,
to serve

Cover the dried split peas with plenty of cold water, cover loosely and leave to soak for a minimum of 12 hours, preferably overnight.

Melt the butter in a heavy-based saucepan, add the garlic and onion and cook for 2–3 minutes, without colouring. Add the rice, drained split peas and tomato purée and cook for 2–3 minutes, stirring continuously to prevent sticking. Add the stock, bring to the boil, then reduce the heat and simmer for 20–25 minutes until the rice and peas are tender. Remove from the heat and leave to cool.

Blend about three quarters of the soup in a food processor or blender to form a smooth purée. Pour the purée into the remaining soup in the saucepan. Add the carrots to the saucepan and cook for a further 10–12 minutes until the carrots are tender.

Meanwhile, place the bacon in a nonstick frying pan and cook over a gentle heat until the bacon is crisp. Remove and drain on absorbent kitchen paper.

Season the soup with salt and pepper to taste, then stir in the parsley and cream. Reheat for 2–3 minutes, then ladle into soup bowls. Sprinkle with the bacon and serve immediately with warm garlic bread.

# Polish Sour Rye Soup

### Serves 4

#### For the ryemeal sour:
75 g/3 oz rye flour
450 ml/15 fl oz lukewarm water

#### For the soup:
225 g/8 oz mixed vegetables, such
as carrots, parsnips and celery,
peeled and chopped
1.7 litres/3 pints water, plus 1 tbsp
225 g/8 oz Polish sausage, chopped
500 g/1 lb 1 oz potatoes
4 tbsp plain flour
1 garlic clove, peeled and crushed
½ tsp salt
hollowed-out cottage loaf, to serve

For the ryemeal sour, mix the rye flour with the lukewarm water and pour into a clean jar large enough for the mixture to expand. Cover with a piece of muslin and leave in a warm place for 4–5 days (or store for up to a week in the refrigerator) until frothy.

For the soup, place the mixed vegetables in a large saucepan. Cover with the 1.7 litres/3 pints water and bring to the boil. Reduce the heat and simmer for 30 minutes.

Add the sausage to the pan and continue to cook for a further 30 minutes. Remove the sausage and leave to cool. When the sausage is cool enough to handle, slice, then return to the pan.

Add the potatoes and ryemeal sour to the pan. Blend the plain flour and 1 tablespoon water together in a bowl. In another bowl, mix the garlic and salt together, then add both to the pan. Bring to the boil, reduce the heat and simmer for 30 minutes, or until the potatoes are tender. Serve in a hollowed-out loaf.

**Cook's Tip:** If liked, cook 2 eggs for 10 minutes, or until hard-boiled. Plunge into cold water and leave until cold. Drain, then shell and cut in half. Place half an egg in each 'loaf bowl' before serving.

# Pasta & Bean Soup

## Serves 4–6

3 tbsp olive oil
2 celery stalks, trimmed and finely chopped
100 g/3¹/₂ oz prosciutto or prosciutto di speck, cut into pieces
1 red chilli, deseeded and finely chopped
2 large potatoes, peeled and cut into 2.5 cm/1 inch cubes
2 garlic cloves, peeled and finely chopped
3 ripe plum tomatoes, skinned and chopped
400 g can borlotti beans, drained and rinsed
1 litre/1³/₄ pints chicken or vegetable stock
100 g/3¹/₂ oz pasta shapes
large handful basil leaves, torn
salt and freshly ground black pepper
shredded basil leaves, to garnish
crusty bread, to serve

Heat the olive oil in a heavy-based pan, add the celery and prosciutto and cook gently for 6–8 minutes until softened. Add the chopped chilli and potato cubes and cook for a further 10 minutes.

Add the garlic to the chilli and potato mixture and cook for 1 minute. Add the chopped tomatoes and simmer for 5 minutes. Stir in two thirds of the beans, then pour in the chicken or vegetable stock and bring to the boil.

Add the pasta shapes to the soup stock and return it to simmering point. Cook the pasta for about 10 minutes until *al dente*.

Meanwhile, place the remaining beans in a food processor or blender and blend with enough of the soup stock to make a smooth, thinnish purée.

When the pasta is cooked, stir in the puréed beans with the torn basil. Season the soup to taste with salt and pepper. Ladle into serving bowls, garnish with shredded basil and serve immediately with plenty of crusty bread.

# Läghmän Noodle Soup

## Serves 4

2 tbsp vegetable oil
450 g/1 lb lean braising steak, cut into small pieces
4 garlic cloves, peeled and sliced
1 medium onion, peeled and sliced
4 baby or small turnips, peeled and chopped
1 carrot, peeled and sliced
1 green or red chilli, deseeded (optional) and sliced
1 red pepper, deseeded and cut into strips
2 tbsp tomato puree
1.7 litres/3 pints beef or chicken stock
2 tbsp rice wine vinegar (optional)
350 g/12 oz läghmän noodles or other Chinese wheat noodles
salt and freshly ground black pepper
1 tbsp shredded basil, to garnish
flat breads, to serve

Heat the oil in a large saucepan, add the beef and fry, stirring, until sealed all over. Add the garlic, onion, turnips and carrot and continue to fry for 10 minutes, or until the vegetables are beginning to soften.

Add the chilli and red pepper to the pan and stir. Blend the tomato purée with a little stock and stir into the pan. Add the remaining stock and the vinegar, if using. Bring to the boil, reduce the heat and simmer for 30 minutes, or until the meat is tender.

Meanwhile, cook the pasta in plenty of boiling water for 10–15 minutes, or according to the packet instructions. Drain, then add to the meat soup. Adjust the seasoning, then divide the soup between warmed bowls, garnish with basil and serve with flat breads.

**Cook's Tip:** Try using short lengths of spaghetti, macaroni or even farfalle, if liked.

# Winter Hotchpot

small piece gammon,
about 300 g/11 oz
1 tbsp olive oil
1 large onion, peeled and
finely chopped
2–3 garlic cloves, peeled and
finely chopped
225 g/8 oz carrots, peeled and
finely chopped
2 celery stalks, trimmed and
finely sliced
175 g/6 oz leeks, trimmed and
finely sliced
1.1 litres/2 pints ham or
vegetable stock
125 g/4 oz pearl barley, rinsed
freshly ground black pepper
crusty bread, to serve

Remove any rind and fat from the gammon and cut into small pieces.

Heat the oil in a large saucepan over a medium heat and add all the prepared vegetables and gammon. Cook, stirring occasionally, for 5–8 minutes until the vegetables have softened.

Pour in the stock and bring to the boil. Cover with a lid and simmer for 10 minutes. Add the pearl barley to the pan.

Continue to simmer, covered, for 15–20 minutes until the vegetables and gammon are tender. Add freshly ground black pepper to taste, then serve with crusty bread.

# Bulgarian Meatball Soup

## Serves 4–6

350 g/12 oz fresh lean beef mince
2 shallots, peeled and
finely chopped
2 tbsp freshly chopped dill
1 medium egg
2 garlic cloves, peeled and finely
chopped or crushed
salt and freshly ground
black pepper
1 tbsp plain flour
1.1 litres/2 pints good beef stock
125 g/4 oz long-grain rice
juice of 1 lemon
bread, to serve

Place the beef mince, shallots, 1 tablespoon chopped dill, egg, garlic and seasoning to taste in a bowl and, using damp hands, bring the ingredients together to form a ball in the centre of the bowl.

Shape the beef mixture into small balls about the size of a small apricot and roll in the flour.

Bring the beef stock to the boil in a large saucepan, then drop in the meatballs. Add the rice, then reduce the heat and simmer for 35 minutes.

Add the lemon juice and the remaining dill, then serve with bread.

**Cook's Tip:** When choosing the beef mince, look for the leanest you can find. Alternatively, buy braising steak or even topside and ask the butcher to mince it for you.

# Venison Ragout Soup

## Serves 4

1 tbsp olive oil
2 medium onions, peeled
and chopped
1 garlic clove, peeled and chopped
1 red chilli, deseeded and
finely chopped
1 leek, trimmed and chopped
450 g/12 oz venison steak, cut into
small pieces
400 g can chopped tomatoes
225 g/8 oz potatoes, peeled
and diced
450 ml/³/₄ pint water
1 tbsp soft brown sugar
salt and freshly ground black pepper
1 tsp hot pepper sauce, or to taste
200 g canned white asparagus,
drained and cut into short lengths
2 tbsp black olives
bread, to serve

## To garnish:

parsley sprigs
dried red chilli flakes (optional)

Heat the oil in a large saucepan, add the onions, garlic, chilli and leek and cook for 5 minutes, stirring, until the onion has begun to soften.

Add the venison and continue to cook, stirring, for 5 minutes, or until the venison is sealed all over.

Add all the remaining ingredients except for the asparagus and olives and bring to the boil. Reduce the heat, cover with a lid and simmer for 50–60 minutes until tender, stirring occasionally. If the liquid is evaporating too quickly, reduce the heat a little and add some more stock.

Add the asparagus to the saucepan with the olives and cook for a further 5–8 minutes until piping hot. Divide the soup between warmed bowls, garnish with parsley and chilli flakes, if liked, and serve with bread.

**Cook's Tip:** If fresh asparagus is available, then use this instead of the canned. Cook the fresh asparagus in lightly boiling water for 5–8 minutes, drain, cool and slice, then use as above.

# Rice Soup with Potato Sticks

## Serves 4

175 g/6 oz butter
1 tsp olive oil
1 large onion, peeled and
finely chopped
4 slices Parma ham, chopped
100 g/3¹/₂ oz arborio rice
1.1 litres/2 pints chicken stock
350 g/12 oz frozen peas
salt and freshly ground
black pepper
1 medium egg
125 g/4 oz self-raising flour
pinch salt
175 g/6 oz mashed potato
1 tbsp milk
1 tbsp poppy seeds
1 tbsp Parmesan cheese,
finely grated
1 tbsp freshly chopped parsley

Preheat the oven to 190°C/375°F/Gas Mark 5. Heat 25 g/1 oz of the butter and the olive oil in a saucepan and cook the onion for 4–5 minutes until softened, then add the Parma ham and cook for about 1 minute. Stir in the rice, the stock and the peas. Season to taste with salt and pepper and simmer for 10–15 minutes until the rice is tender.

Beat the egg and 125 g/4 oz of the butter together until smooth, then beat in the flour, a pinch of salt and the potato. Work the ingredients together to form a soft, pliable dough, adding a little more flour if necessary.

Roll the dough out on a lightly floured surface into a rectangle 1 cm/¹/₂ inch thick and cut into 12 thin, long sticks. Brush with milk and sprinkle on the poppy seeds. Place the sticks on a lightly oiled baking tray and bake in the preheated oven for 15 minutes, or until golden.

When the rice is cooked, stir the remaining butter and Parmesan cheese into the soup and sprinkle the chopped parsley over the top. Serve immediately with the warm potato sticks.

# Pork Dumplings ❧ Cabbage Soup

## Serves 4

225 g/8 oz green cabbage, outer
leaves and hard core discarded,
plus extra blanched leaves to serve

1 1/4 tsp salt

225 g/8 oz fresh lean pork mince

1 small egg white

1 tsp cornflour

1/2 tsp ground white pepper

1/2 tsp soft brown sugar

1 tsp white wine vinegar

3 spring onions, trimmed
and chopped

24 wonton wrappers

1.1 litres/2 pints chicken stock

1 tsp sesame oil, plus extra to
serve (optional)

caramelised onion (*see* page 180) to
garnish (optional)

Shred the cabbage very finely (if preferred, use a food processor), then place in a bowl and sprinkle with the 1/4 teaspoon salt. Leave in a warm room for 30 minutes. Drain well, squeezing out the water that has come out of the cabbage.

Mix the shredded cabbage with the pork mince, 1 teaspoon salt, egg white, cornflour, pepper, sugar, vinegar and one of the chopped spring onions.

Holding a wonton wrapper in one hand, moisten half of one edge lightly with water. Place a spoonful of the mixture in the wrapper and pinch up the edges to seal. Repeat with the remaining wrappers and pork mixture (remember to cover the wrappers with a tea towel while working to keep them moist).

Heat the chicken stock and the sesame oil. Drop 3–4 filled dumplings into the stock and cook for 2–4 minutes until cooked. Remove and drain on kitchen paper. Repeat with the remaining dumplings. To serve, place 3–4 dumplings in a bowl, add a drop of sesame oil if liked with some blanched cabbage and some caramelised onions, if using.

# Rassolnik (Russian Pickled Cucumber Soup)

### Serves 4

450 g/1 lb stewing or braising beef
1.7 litres/3 pints water
2 small onions, peeled and chopped
2 tbsp vegetable oil
1 large carrot, peeled and chopped
2 celery stalks, trimmed and chopped
1 medium tomato, chopped
2 large pickled cucumbers, chopped
1 large potato, peeled and chopped
2 tbsp freshly chopped parsley
1 carrot, peeled and finely diced, to garnish

### To serve:

sour cream
crusty bread

Place the beef in a saucepan, cover with the water and add one of the onions. Bring to the boil, then reduce the heat, cover with a lid and simmer for 1 hour, removing any scum that rises to the top. Remove from the heat and leave to cool. When cool enough to handle, cut the beef into small pieces. Strain the beef broth, discarding the onion and reserve.

Heat the oil in a frying pan, add the remaining onion, the carrot and celery and fry for 15 minutes, or until beginning to soften. Add the chopped tomato and cook for a further 5 minutes.

Place the pickled cucumbers in a medium saucepan and add the reserved beef broth. Bring to the boil, then reduce the heat and simmer for 20 minutes. Add the chopped beef with the cooked vegetables and potato to the cucumber, then heat for a further 15 minutes, or until piping hot. Sprinkle with the parsley and diced carrot and serve with sour cream and bread.

# Poultry

With recipes featuring chicken, duck and turkey, the soups in this chapter offer a tempting array of tastes and textures for poultry fans. The Chicken Tortilla Soup will delight with its combination of Mexican-flavoured chicken and crunchy tortillas, whilst Thai Duck Noodle Soup is a wealth of tasty goodness. Alongside comforting and wholesome classics like Cream of Chicken Soup, there is every reason to put soup on the menu!

# Chicken Tortilla Soup

## Serves 4

about 900 ml/1¹/₂ pints
chicken stock
2 tbsp lime juice
400 g can chopped tomatoes
1 red chilli, deseeded and chopped
125 g/4 oz canned mild green
chillies, drained and halved
or chopped
1 large carrot, peeled
and chopped
1 onion, peeled and chopped
75 g/3 oz sweetcorn kernels
3 tbsp sunflower or vegetable oil
3 corn tortillas, cut into strips
225 g/8 oz cooked chicken meat
75 g/3 oz hard cheese, such as
Cheddar, grated
1 tbsp freshly chopped coriander
salt and freshly ground
black pepper
lime wedges, to serve

Pour the chicken stock into a large saucepan, then add the lime juice, tomatoes, all the chillies, the carrot, onion and sweetcorn. Bring to the boil, reduce the heat, cover with a lid and simmer for 45 minutes. If the liquid is evaporating too quickly, reduce the heat a little and add a little extra stock if necessary.

Meanwhile, heat the oil in a frying pan and fry the tortilla strips for 2–3 minutes until crisp. Drain on kitchen paper and reserve.

Cut the chicken into bite-size pieces and add to the pan together with the cheese, coriander and seasoning to taste. Heat for 5–8 minutes until the chicken is piping hot. Serve in bowls with the fried tortilla strips and lime wedges.

**Cook's Tip:** Pickled chillies can be found in cans or jars in the deli counter. Any unused chillies can be kept in a small covered bowl in the refrigerator.

# Clear Chicken & Mushroom Soup

### Serves 4

2 large chicken legs, about
450 g/1 lb total weight
1 tbsp groundnut oil
1 tsp sesame oil
1 onion, peeled and very thinly sliced
2.5 cm/1 inch piece root ginger,
peeled and very finely chopped
1.1 litres/2 pints clear chicken stock
1 lemongrass stalk, bruised
50 g/2 oz long-grain rice
75 g/3 oz button mushrooms, wiped
and finely sliced
4 spring onions, trimmed, cut into
5 cm/2 inch pieces and shredded
1 tbsp dark soy sauce
4 tbsp dry sherry
salt and freshly ground
black pepper

Skin the chicken legs and remove any fat. Cut each in half to make two thigh and two drumstick portions and reserve. Heat the groundnut and sesame oils in a large saucepan. Add the sliced onion and cook gently for 10 minutes, or until soft but not beginning to colour.

Add the chopped ginger to the saucepan and cook for about 30 seconds, stirring all the time to prevent it sticking, then pour in the stock. Add the chicken pieces and the lemongrass, cover and simmer gently for 15 minutes. Stir in the rice and cook for a further 15 minutes, or until the chicken is cooked.

Remove the chicken from the saucepan and leave until cool enough to handle. Finely shred the flesh, then return to the saucepan with the mushrooms, spring onions, soy sauce and sherry. Simmer for 5 minutes, or until the rice and mushrooms are tender. Remove the lemongrass.

Season the soup to taste with salt and pepper. Ladle into warmed serving bowls, making sure each has an equal amount of shredded chicken and vegetables, and serve immediately.

# Moroccan Couscous Soup

1.1 litres/2 pints chicken stock
$\frac{1}{2}$ tsp ground cumin
1 onion, peeled and chopped
3 garlic cloves, peeled and crushed
1 large carrot, peeled and chopped
1 celery stalk, trimmed and chopped
1 tbsp vegetable oil
350 g/12 oz chicken meat, preferably breast, cut into small pieces
1 tsp ground coriander
$\frac{1}{2}$ tsp ground cinnamon
4 whole cloves
400 g can chopped tomatoes
2–3 coriander sprigs
125 g/4 oz couscous
salt and freshly ground black pepper

Pour the stock into a medium saucepan and add the cumin, onion, garlic, carrot and celery. Bring to the boil, then reduce the heat and simmer for 15 minutes.

Heat the oil in a frying pan, add the chicken and all the remaining spices and fry for 5–8 minutes, stirring frequently, until the chicken is sealed and coated in the spices. Drain and reserve.

Stir the tomatoes into the stock and add the coriander, reserving a little for the garnish, and the chicken. Bring to the boil, then cover with a lid, reduce the heat and simmer for 10–12 minutes until the chicken is cooked. Season to taste with salt and pepper.

Cook the couscous according to the packet instructions, or place in a bowl and cover with hot water. Leave for 10 minutes, or until the water has been absorbed, then fluff with a fork.

Divide the couscous among four bowls and add the soup. Garnish with the remaining coriander sprigs and serve.

**Cook's Tip:** Use either stock cubes or fresh chicken stock if liked, according to how much time you have.

# Creamy Chicken & Tofu Soup

### Serves 4

225 g/8 oz firm tofu, drained
3 tbsp groundnut oil
1 garlic clove, peeled and crushed
2.5 cm/1 inch piece root ginger,
peeled and finely chopped
2.5 cm/1 inch piece fresh galangal,
peeled and finely sliced
(if available)
1 lemongrass stalk, bruised
1/4 tsp ground turmeric
600 ml/1 pint chicken stock
600 ml/1 pint coconut milk
225 g/8 oz cauliflower, cut into
tiny florets
1 medium carrot, peeled and cut
into thin matchsticks
125 g/4 oz green beans, trimmed
and cut in half
75 g/3 oz thin egg noodles
225 g/8 oz cooked chicken,
shredded
salt and freshly ground
black pepper

Cut the tofu into 1 cm/1/2 inch cubes, then pat dry on absorbent kitchen paper.

Heat 1 tablespoon of the oil in a nonstick frying pan. Fry the tofu in two batches for 3–4 minutes until golden brown. Remove, drain on absorbent kitchen paper and reserve.

Heat the remaining oil in a large saucepan. Add the garlic, ginger, galangal and lemon grass and cook for about 30 seconds. Stir in the turmeric, then pour in the stock and coconut milk and bring to the boil. Reduce the heat to a gentle simmer, add the cauliflower and carrot and simmer for 10 minutes. Add the green beans and simmer for a further 5 minutes.

Meanwhile, bring a large saucepan of lightly salted water to the boil. Add the noodles, turn off the heat, cover and leave to cook, or cook according to the packet instructions.

Remove the lemongrass from the soup. Drain the noodles and stir into the soup with the chicken and browned tofu. Season to taste with salt and pepper, then simmer gently for 2–3 minutes until heated through. Serve immediately in warmed soup bowls.

# Chicken Pho Soup

125 g/4 oz dried fine noodles
1.1 litres/2 pints chicken stock
1 tbsp freshly grated root ginger
1 garlic clove, peeled and crushed
2 whole star anise
2 tbsp fish sauce
1 tbsp soy sauce
2 tbsp lime juice
225 g/8 oz cooked chicken meat,
finely shredded
4 spring onions, trimmed and
finely shredded
75 g/3 oz beansprouts
2 tbsp roughly chopped parsley

Soak the dried noodles in hot water for 10 minutes, or according to the packet instructions. Drain and reserve.

Pour the chicken stock into a wok or large saucepan and add the ginger, garlic and the star anise. Bring to a simmer and cook for 5 minutes, then add the fish and soy sauces and lime juice and simmer for a further 5 minutes.

Add the chicken with the spring onions and drained noodles. Simmer for a further 5 minutes, then add the beansprouts. Heat for 5 minutes before adding the parsley and serving.

# Wonton Soup

## Serves 4

### For the chicken stock:

900 g/2 lb chicken or chicken pieces with back, feet and wings
1–2 onions, peeled and quartered
2 carrots, peeled and chopped
2 celery stalks, trimmed and chopped
1 leek, trimmed and chopped
2 garlic cloves, unpeeled and lightly crushed
1 tbsp black peppercorns
2 bay leaves
small bunch parsley, stems only
2–3 slices fresh root ginger, peeled (optional)
3.4 litres/6 pints cold water

### For the soup:

18 wontons; 2–3 Chinese leaves, or a handful of spinach, shredded; 1 small carrot, peeled and cut into matchsticks; 2–4 spring onions, trimmed and diagonally sliced; soy sauce, to taste; handful flat-leaf parsley

Chop the chicken into 6–8 pieces and put into a large stock pot or saucepan of water with the remaining stock ingredients. Place over a high heat and bring to the boil, skimming off any scum which rises to the surface. Reduce the heat and simmer for 2–3 hours, skimming occasionally.

Strain the stock through a fine sieve or muslin-lined sieve into a large bowl. Leave to cool, then chill in the refrigerator for 5–6 hours, or overnight. When cold, skim off the fat and remove any small pieces of fat by dragging a piece of absorbent kitchen paper lightly across the surface.

Bring a medium saucepan of water to the boil. Add the wontons and return to the boil. Simmer for 2–3 minutes until the wontons are cooked, stir frequently. Rinse under cold running water, drain and reserve.

Pour 300 ml/$\frac{1}{2}$ pint stock per person into a large wok. Bring to the boil over a high heat, skimming any foam that rises to the surface, and simmer for 5–7 minutes to reduce slightly. Add the wontons, Chinese leaves or spinach, carrot and spring onions. Season with a few drops of soy sauce and simmer for 2–3 minutes. Garnish with a few parsley leaves and serve immediately.

# Thai Duck Noodle Soup

### Serves 4

### For the stock:

1 duck carcass or 1 duck leg; 1.1 litres/2 pints water; 1 cinnamon stick; 2 whole star anise; small piece root ginger; 1 small onion, peeled and chopped; 1 celery stalk, trimmed and chopped; 1 whole garlic clove, peeled; few thyme sprigs, or use 1 tsp dried; 1 fresh bay leaf

### For the soup:

1.1 litres/2 pints duck stock, or use chicken
1–3 red bird's-eye chillies, deseeded and chopped
1 cinnamon stick, lightly bruised
2 whole star anise
2 tbsp soy sauce
1–2 tsp sweet chilli sauce, or to taste
175 g/6 oz fine dried noodles, soaked for 10 minutes in hot water
175 g/6 oz cooked duck, shredded
6 spring onions, trimmed and chopped
125 g/4 oz beansprouts
freshly chopped parsley, for sprinkling

Place the carcass or duck leg in a wok or large saucepan and add the water with all the other stock ingredients. Bring to the boil, then reduce the heat and simmer for 1 hour. If the liquid is evaporating too quickly, add some extra water and reduce the heat. Reserve.

When ready to make the soup, strain the stock and return to the rinsed-out wok or pan. Add all the soup ingredients except for the noodles, duck, spring onions and beansprouts. Bring to the boil, then reduce the heat and simmer for 10 minutes before adding the noodles, duck, spring onions and beansprouts. Simmer for a further 10 minutes, then serve sprinkled with chopped parsley.

**Cook's Tip:** Beware of the red and green bird's-eye chillies. Although they are very small, they are extremely hot to eat. When deseeding, remove the membrane that the chilli seeds are attached to, as this is as hot in the mouth as the seeds are. After handling the chillies, wash your hands and equipment thoroughly and do not touch your face or other sensitive areas until you have washed your hands.

# Creamy Caribbean Chicken & Coconut Soup

### Serves 4

6–8 spring onions
2 garlic cloves
1 red chilli
175 g/6 oz cooked chicken, shredded or diced
2 tbsp vegetable oil
1 tsp ground turmeric
300 ml/$^1$/$_2$ pint coconut milk
900 ml/1$^1$/$_2$ pints chicken stock
50 g/2 oz small soup pasta or spaghetti, broken into small pieces
$^1$/$_2$ lemon, sliced
salt and freshly ground black pepper
1–2 tbsp freshly chopped coriander
fresh coriander sprigs, to garnish

Trim the spring onions and slice thinly; peel the garlic and chop finely. Cut off the top from the chilli, slit down the side and remove seeds and membrane, then chop finely and reserve.

Remove and discard any skin or bones from the cooked chicken and shred using two forks and reserve.

Heat a large wok, add the oil and, when hot, add the spring onions, garlic and chilli and stir-fry for 2 minutes, or until the onion has softened. Stir in the turmeric and cook for 1 minute.

Blend the coconut milk with the chicken stock until smooth, then pour into the wok. Add the pasta or spaghetti with the lemon slices and bring to the boil. Simmer, half-covered, for 10–12 minutes until the pasta is tender; stir occasionally.

Remove the lemon slices from the wok and add the chicken. Season to taste with salt and pepper and simmer for 2–3 minutes until the chicken is heated through thoroughly.

Stir in the chopped coriander and ladle into heated bowls. Garnish with sprigs of fresh coriander and serve immediately.

# Wild Rice & Chicken Soup

### Serves 4

125 g/4 oz wild rice
$^1/_2$ tsp salt
450 ml/$^3/_4$ pint water
2 tbsp butter
300 g/11 oz skinless, boneless
chicken breasts, cut into
small pieces
2 medium onions, peeled
and chopped
2 garlic cloves, peeled
and chopped
1 celery stalk, trimmed and sliced,
reserve some leaves to garnish
2 tbsp plain flour
900 ml/1$^1/_2$ pints chicken stock
1 bouquet garni
salt and freshly ground
black pepper
150 ml/$^1/_4$ pint single cream
fresh herbs, to garnish (optional)
toasted ciabatta bread, to serve

Rinse the rice and place in a saucepan with $^1/_2$ teaspoon salt and the water. Bring to the boil, reduce the heat, cover with a lid and simmer for 40 minutes, stirring occasionally, and adding more water if necessary. When the rice is cooked, drain and reserve.

Heat the butter in a large saucepan, add the chicken and fry, stirring, for 10–12 minutes until sealed and lightly browned. Add the vegetables and fry for a further 5 minutes. Sprinkle in the flour and cook for 2 minutes. Remove the pan from the heat and gradually stir in the stock. Return to the heat and cook, stirring, for 2 minutes. Add the bouquet garni and cover with a lid.

Reduce the heat and simmer for 15 minutes. Add the wild rice and cook for a further 5 minutes. Add seasoning to taste, stir in the cream and heat for another 2 minutes before ladling into warmed soup bowls. Garnish with celery leaves or herbs, if liked, and serve with toasted ciabatta bread.

**Cook's Tip:** If liked, use skinless, boneless chicken thighs and cook for at least 12 extra minutes to ensure that the chicken is cooked and tender.

# Hot-⚜-Sour Soup

## Serves 4–6

25 g/1 oz dried Chinese (shiitake) mushrooms
2 tbsp groundnut oil
1 carrot, peeled and cut into strips
125 g/4 oz chestnut mushrooms, wiped and thinly sliced
2 garlic cloves, peeled and chopped
1/2 tsp dried crushed chillies
1.1 litres/2 pints chicken stock (*see* p. 88)
75 g/3 oz cooked boneless chicken or pork, shredded
125 g/4 oz fresh tofu, thinly sliced, (optional)
2–3 spring onions, trimmed and finely sliced diagonally
1–2 tsp sugar
3 tbsp cider vinegar
2 tbsp soy sauce
salt and freshly ground black pepper
1 tbsp cornflour
1 large egg
2 tsp sesame oil
2 tbsp freshly chopped coriander

Place the dried Chinese (shiitake) mushrooms in a small bowl and pour over enough almost-boiling water to cover. Leave for 20 minutes to soften, then gently lift out and squeeze out the liquid. (Lifting out the mushrooms leaves any sand and grit behind.) Discard the stems and thinly slice the caps and reserve.

Heat a large wok, add the oil and, when hot, add the carrot strips and stir-fry for 2–3 minutes until beginning to soften. Add the chestnut mushrooms and stir-fry for 2–3 minutes until golden, then stir in the garlic and chillies.

Add the chicken stock to the vegetables and bring to the boil, skimming off any foam which rises to the surface. Add the shredded chicken or pork, tofu, if using, spring onions, sugar, vinegar, soy sauce and reserved Chinese mushrooms and simmer for 5 minutes, stirring occasionally. Season to taste with salt and pepper.

Blend the cornflour with 1 tablespoon cold water to form a smooth paste and whisk into the soup. Return to the boil and simmer over a medium heat until thickened. Beat the egg with the sesame oil and gradually add to the soup in a slow, steady stream, stirring continuously. Stir in the chopped coriander and serve the soup immediately.

# Avgolemono
# (Egg-Lemon Soup)

## Serves 6

1. 5 kg/3 lb whole oven-ready
chicken
about 2.25 litres/4 pints water
2 tbsp sunflower oil
1 onion, peeled and finely chopped
1 large carrot, peeled and
roughly chopped
1 large leek, trimmed
2 bay leaves
175 g/6 oz arborio rice
2 medium eggs
4 tbsp freshly squeezed lemon juice
salt and freshly ground black pepper
1 tbsp freshly chopped parsley

Wipe the chicken cavity with a damp cloth or kitchen paper, then place in a large saucepan and cover with the water. Bring to the boil over a medium heat, then cover with a lid, reduce the heat and simmer for 1 hour, or until tender. Remove from the heat and leave to cool.

When the chicken is cool enough to handle, remove from the stock and take the chicken from the bones. Discard the skin and cut the meat into bite-size pieces. Reserve.

Heat the oil in a frying pan, add all the vegetables and fry for 10 minutes, stirring frequently, then add to the chicken stock in the saucepan together with the bay leaves and rice. Bring to the boil, then reduce the heat and simmer for a further 30 minutes, or until the rice is tender. Add the chicken to the saucepan.

Beat the eggs with the lemon juice and pour in about 150 ml/$1/4$ pint of the warm stock, stirring through. Add a further 150 ml/$1/4$ pint of the stock, then carefully pour this into the saucepan, stirring all the time. Season to taste with salt and pepper and serve garnished with the chopped parsley.

**Cook's Tip:** Take care when adding the egg and lemon juice to the soup, otherwise the egg may curdle.

# Laksa Malaysian Rice Noodle Soup

## Serves 4

1.1 kg/2½ lb corn-fed chicken
1 tsp black peppercorns
1 tbsp vegetable oil
1 large onion, peeled and thinly sliced
2 garlic cloves, peeled and finely chopped
2.5 cm/1 inch piece fresh root ginger, peeled and thinly sliced
1 tsp ground coriander
2 red chillies, deseeded and diagonally sliced
1–2 tsp hot curry paste
400 ml/14 fl oz coconut milk
450 g/1 lb large raw prawns, peeled and deveined
½ small head Chinese leaves, thinly shredded
1 tsp sugar
2 spring onions, trimmed and sliced
125 g/4 oz beansprouts
250 g/9 oz rice noodles or rice sticks, soaked as per packet instructions
fresh mint leaves, to garnish

Put the chicken in a large saucepan with the peppercorns and cover with cold water. Bring to the boil, skimming off any scum that rises to the surface. Simmer, partially covered, for about 1 hour. Remove the chicken and cool. Skim any fat from the stock and strain through a muslin-lined sieve and reserve. Remove the meat from the carcass, shred and reserve.

Heat a large wok, add the oil and, when hot, add the onions and stir-fry for 2 minutes, or until they begin to colour. Stir in the garlic, ginger, coriander, chillies and curry paste and stir-fry for a further 2 minutes.

Carefully pour in the reserved stock (you need at least 1.1 litres/ 2 pints) and simmer gently, partially covered, for 10 minutes, or until slightly reduced.

Add the coconut milk, prawns, Chinese leaves, sugar, spring onions and beansprouts and simmer for 3 minutes, stirring occasionally. Add the reserved shredded chicken and cook for a further 2 minutes.

Drain the noodles and divide between four soup bowls. Ladle the hot stock and vegetables over the noodles, making sure each serving has some prawns and chicken. Garnish each bowl with fresh mint leaves and serve immediately.

# Cock-o-Leekie Soup

## Serves 6

1. 5 kg/3 lb whole oven-ready chicken
about 2.25 litres/4 pints water
2 large onions, peeled and finely chopped
2 large carrots, peeled and roughly chopped
2 leeks, trimmed and chopped
1 fresh bouquet garni or 2 fresh bay leaves
125 g/4 oz sweetcorn kernels
15 ready-to-eat prunes

## For clarifying:
2 egg whites
175 g/6 oz minced chicken (mince meat from the cooked chicken)

Preheat the oven to 190°C/375°F/Gas Mark 5, 15 minutes before cooking. Place the chicken in a roasting tin and roast in the oven for 30 minutes. Remove the chicken and place in a large saucepan, cover with the water, half the vegetables and the bouquet garni. Bring to the boil, then reduce the heat and simmer for 1–1¹/₂ hours until the chicken is cooked. Remove from the heat and leave to cool.

When the chicken is cool enough to handle, remove from the stock and discard the skin and bones. Cut the meat into strips and strain the stock. Place the stock into a clean pan and bring to the boil.

Beat the egg whites and minced chicken together, then slowly whisk into the stock. Continue to whisk until the minced chicken rises to the surface. Remove and strain the stock again into a clean pan. Add the remaining uncooked vegetables together with the chicken meat, sweetcorn and prunes and heat over a medium heat until piping hot, then serve.

**Cook's Tip:** This is a traditional Scottish meal; the soup is often served on its own as a first course with a little of the cooked chicken, and the rest of the cooked chicken is served separately as the main course.

# Chicken Noodle Soup

## Serves 4

carcass of a medium-size
cooked chicken
1 large carrot, peeled and
roughly chopped
1 medium onion, peeled
and quartered
1 leek, trimmed and
roughly chopped
2–3 bay leaves
few black peppercorns
2 litres/3¹/₂ pints water
225 g/8 oz Chinese
cabbage, trimmed
50 g/2 oz chestnut mushrooms,
wiped and sliced
125 g/4 oz cooked chicken, sliced
or chopped
50 g/2 oz medium or fine egg
thread noodles

Break the chicken carcass into smaller pieces and place in the wok with the carrot, onion, leek, bay leaves, peppercorns and water. Bring slowly to the boil. Skim away any fat or scum that rises for the first 15 minutes. Simmer very gently for 1–1¹/₂ hours. If the liquid reduces by more than one third, add a little more water.

Remove from the heat and leave until cold. Strain into a large bowl and chill in the refrigerator until any fat in the stock rises and sets on the surface. Remove the fat and discard. Draw a sheet of absorbent kitchen paper across the surface of the stock to absorb any remaining fat.

Return the stock to the wok and bring to a simmer. Add the Chinese cabbage, mushrooms and chicken and simmer gently for 7–8 minutes until the vegetables are tender.

Meanwhile, cook the noodles according to the packet instructions until tender. Drain well. Transfer a portion of noodles to each serving bowl before pouring in some soup and vegetables. Serve immediately.

# Cream of Chicken Soup

Serves 4

1 tbsp olive oil
450 g/1 lb skinless, boneless
chicken, such as thighs and
breast fillets
300 ml/½ pint white wine
1 onion, peeled and chopped
1 large carrot, peeled
and chopped
1 celery stalk, trimmed
and chopped
1 fresh bouquet garni
3 parsley sprigs, plus extra
chopped parsley to garnish
1.1 litres/2 pints water
50 g/2 oz butter
50 g/2 oz plain flour
salt and freshly ground
black pepper
300 ml/½ pint single cream

Heat the oil in a frying pan, add the chicken and fry until the chicken is browned all over. Remove the chicken from the pan and place in a large saucepan. Pour in the wine, bring to the boil and boil for 4 minutes.

Add all the vegetables with the bouquet garni and the parsley sprigs, then pour in the water. Bring to the boil, reduce the heat, cover with a lid and simmer for 40 minutes, or until the chicken is tender. Remove from the heat and leave to cool.

When cool enough to handle, discard the bouquet garni, then remove the chicken from the pan. Whizz the stock and vegetables in a food processor until smooth and reserve.

Take the chicken off the bones and cut the meat into small pieces. Clean the saucepan, then add the butter and allow to melt before stirring in the flour. Draw off the heat and slowly stir in the stock. Return to the heat and cook, stirring, until the soup thickens. Stir in the chicken, add seasoning to taste and heat, stirring occasionally, for 10 minutes, then slowly add the cream. Heat for 5 minutes, then serve with a little parsley sprinkled over the top.

# Mexican Soup

### Serves 4

2 cooked boneless chicken breasts,
2 tbsp olive oil
1 onion, peeled and chopped
2 garlic cloves, peeled and crushed
1 large dried chilli, soaked in warm
water for 15 minutes
1–2 red chillies, deseeded
and chopped
½ tsp ground cumin
400 g can chopped tomatoes
900 ml/1½ pints chicken stock
4 tbsp fresh lime juice
salt and freshly ground black pepper
1 ripe avocado
50 g/2 oz pitted black olives
1 tbsp freshly chopped coriander

Cut the chicken into small strips and reserve. Heat the oil in a medium saucepan and, when hot, fry the chicken until golden, remove and reserve. Add the onion, garlic and both the dried and fresh chillies to the pan and fry for 2 minutes. Add the cumin and fry for a further 2 minutes. Add the tomatoes to the pan, then stir in the stock. Whizz in batches in a food processor until smooth, then return to a clean saucepan.

Add the chicken to the pan and bring to the boil. Reduce the heat and simmer for 15 minutes, or until the chicken is piping hot.

Stir the lime juice into the soup with seasoning to taste. Peel the avocado and remove and discard the stone. Chop the flesh and add to the soup with the olives. Sprinkle with the coriander and serve.

**Cook's Tip:** When using avocados in cooking, prepare just before using, otherwise they will go brown. However, if liked, the peeled avocado can be lightly tossed in lemon or lime juice to prevent them browning. Be sure to use only a little lime juice, as too much could alter the taste of the finished dish.

# Chinese Chicken Soup

Serves 4

225 g/8 oz cooked chicken
1 tsp groundnut or vegetable oil
6 spring onions, trimmed and
diagonally sliced
1 red chilli, deseeded and
finely chopped
1 garlic clove, peeled and crushed
2.5 cm/1 inch piece
root ginger, peeled and finely grated
1 litre/1³/₄ pints chicken stock
150 g/5 oz medium egg noodles
1 carrot, peeled and cut
into matchsticks
125 g/4 oz beansprouts
2 tbsp soy sauce
1 tbsp fish sauce
fresh coriander leaves, to garnish

Remove any skin from the chicken. Place on a chopping board and use two forks to tear the chicken into fine shreds.

Heat the oil in a large saucepan and fry the spring onions and chilli for 1 minute.

Add the garlic and ginger and cook for another minute. Stir in the chicken stock and gradually bring the mixture to the boil.

Break up the noodles a little and add to the boiling stock with the carrot. Stir to mix, then reduce the heat to a simmer and cook for 3–4 minutes.

Add the shredded chicken, beansprouts, soy sauce and fish sauce and stir.

Cook for a further 2–3 minutes until piping hot. Ladle the soup into bowls and sprinkle with the coriander leaves. Serve immediately.

# Tomato Chicken Soup

## Serves 4

2 tbsp vegetable oil
2 medium onions, peeled
and chopped
2 garlic cloves, peeled and crushed
2 medium carrots, peeled
and sliced
2 celery stalks, trimmed and sliced
1.6 litres/2³/₄ pints chicken stock
450 g/1 lb ripe tomatoes, skinned
and chopped
2 bay leaves
1 tbsp tomato purée
350 g/12 oz cooked chicken meat,
cut into small pieces
350 g/12 oz cooked new potatoes,
cut into quarters
salt and freshly ground black pepper
parsley sprigs, to garnish

Heat the oil in a medium saucepan and add 1 onion, 1 garlic clove, 1 carrot and 1 celery stalk. Pour in half the stock, then cook, stirring, for 20 minutes, or until the vegetables are soft. Leave to cool, then pass through a food processor and return to the saucepan.

Add the tomatoes and cook for a further 15 minutes, or until the tomatoes have begun to collapse. Add the bay leaves. Blend the tomato purée with the remaining vegetable stock, pour into the pan and add the chicken and potatoes.

Bring to the boil, reduce the heat and simmer for a further 15–20 minutes until the chicken is piping hot. Season to taste, then serve in warm bowls garnished with parsley.

# Chicken ❧ Potato Soup With Peas

## Serves 4

450 g/1 lb skinless, boneless
chicken breast fillets
6 black peppercorns
small piece celery
1 small carrot, peeled
1 small onion, peeled
1.1 litres/2 pints water, plus
3 tbsp water
350 g/12 oz potatoes, peeled
and chopped
125 g/4 oz fresh peas, shelled
1 tbsp cornflour
4 dill sprigs

## To garnish:

freshly chopped mixed herbs
2 spring onions, chopped
(optional)

Place the chicken in a medium saucepan together with the peppercorns, celery, carrot and onion. Pour in the 1.1 litres/2 pints water, then bring to the boil. Reduce the heat, cover with a lid and simmer for 30 minutes. Remove from the heat and leave to cool.

When cool enough to handle, remove the chicken from the pan and take the meat off the bones. Strain the stock and return to the cleaned pan. Reserve the chicken meat.

Add the potatoes to the pan and bring to the boil. Cover with a lid, reduce the heat and cook for 12 minutes. Add the shelled peas and chicken and continue to cook for a further 10 minutes, or until the potatoes and peas are tender.

Blend the cornflour with the 3 tablespoons water and slowly stir into the soup. Cook for a further 5 minutes, or until the soup thickens slightly and the chicken is piping hot. Add the dill for the last 2 minutes of cooking. Serve hot, garnished with chopped mixed herbs and the spring onions, if using.

# Coconut Chicken Soup

## Serves 4

2 lemongrass stalks
3 tbsp vegetable oil
3 medium onions, peeled and
finely sliced
3 garlic cloves, peeled and crushed
2 tbsp fresh root ginger, finely grated
2–3 kaffir lime leaves
1 1/2 tsp turmeric
1 red pepper, deseeded and diced
400 ml can coconut milk
1.1 litres/2 pints vegetable or
chicken stock
275 g/10 oz easy-cook long-grain rice
275 g/10 oz cooked chicken meat
285 g can sweetcorn, drained
3 tbsp freshly chopped coriander
1 tbsp Thai fish sauce
freshly chopped pickled chillies,
to serve

Discard the outer leaves of the lemongrass stalks, then place on a chopping board and, using a mallet or rolling pin, pound gently to bruise; reserve.

Heat the vegetable oil in a large saucepan and cook the onions over a medium heat for about 10–15 minutes until soft and beginning to change colour.

Lower the heat, stir in the garlic, ginger, lime leaves and turmeric and cook for 1 minute. Add the red pepper, coconut milk, stock, lemongrass and rice. Bring to the boil, cover and simmer gently over a low heat for about 10 minutes.

Cut the chicken into bite-size pieces, then stir into the soup with the sweetcorn and the freshly chopped coriander. Add a few dashes of the Thai fish sauce to taste, then reheat gently, stirring frequently. Serve immediately with a few chopped pickled chillies to sprinkle on top.

# Bulgarian Chicken Soup

## Serves 6

900 g/2 lb skinless, boneless
chicken breast fillets
1 tsp salt
6 black peppercorns
6 parsley sprigs
1.1 litres/2 pints water
2 tbsp vegetable oil or butter
1 onion, peeled and chopped
3 carrots, peeled and chopped
2 celery stalks, trimmed
and chopped
1 tbsp plain flour
1 medium egg
250 ml/8 fl oz milk
freshly ground black pepper
fresh herbs, to garnish

Place the chicken into a medium saucepan and add the salt, peppercorns and half the parsley. Pour in the water and bring to the boil. Reduce the heat and simmer for 30 minutes, or until tender. Remove from the heat and leave until cool enough to handle. Remove the chicken from the water and take the meat off the bones. Discard both the skin and bones and shred the chicken meat. Strain the stock. Reserve both the stock and chicken meat.

Heat the oil or butter, add the vegetables and cook for 8–10 minutes until beginning to soften, stirring occasionally. Sprinkle in the flour and stir well.

Add the chicken together with the strained stock. Bring to the boil, then reduce the heat and simmer for a further 15 minutes.

Beat the egg into the milk, then slowly add to the soup, stirring throughout. Finely chop the remaining parsley and add to the soup. Add the seasoning, garnish with fresh herbs and serve.

# Chicken & Vegetable Soup

### Serves 4

900 g/2 lb assorted skinless
chicken joints
900 ml/1½ pints water
2 medium onions, peeled
and chopped
2 medium carrots, peeled and
roughly chopped
2 celery stalks, trimmed and sliced
1 bouquet garni or 2 bay leaves
8 baby onions, peeled
125 g/4 oz small cauliflower florets
125 g/4 oz Brussels sprouts (optional)
1 red pepper, deseeded and
finely chopped
75 g/3 oz peas, thawed if frozen
salt and freshly ground black pepper
few flat-leaf parsley sprigs, to garnish

Lightly rinse the chicken, then place in a medium saucepan with the water, 1 chopped onion, 1 chopped carrot, 1 sliced celery stalk and the bouquet garni.

Bring to the boil, then cover with a lid, reduce the heat and simmer for 30 minutes, or until the chicken is tender. Remove from the heat and leave to cool.

When cool, remove the chicken and strain the liquid back into the pan. Cut the chicken into small pieces. Reserve.

Add the remaining vegetables except for the red pepper and peas and add seasoning to taste. Bring to the boil, then reduce the heat, cover with a lid and cook gently for 15 minutes. Add the peas with the chicken and continue to cook for a further 15 minutes, or until the chicken is piping hot and the vegetables are tender. Serve garnished with parsley.

**Cook's Tip:** Vary the vegetables according to personal preference and availability.

# Turkey & Dumpling Soup

## Serves 6

### For the soup:

350 g/12 oz skinless, boneless turkey
breast fillet or steaks
2 tbsp olive oil
2 medium onions, peeled and chopped
2 medium carrots, peeled and chopped
1 medium parsnip, peeled and
roughly chopped
1 yellow pepper, deseeded
and chopped
2 fresh bay leaves
1.1 litres/2 pints turkey or chicken stock
1 tbsp tomato purée
salt and freshly ground black pepper
225 g/8 oz tomatoes, skinned
and chopped
crusty bread, to serve

### For the dumplings:

125 g/4 oz plain flour
salt and freshly ground black pepper
50 g/2 oz shredded suet
$^1$/$_2$ tsp baking powder
2–3 tbsp water

Cut the turkey into pieces. Heat the oil in a frying pan, add the turkey and fry, stirring frequently, for 5 minutes, or until sealed. Place in a large saucepan together with the onions, carrots, parsnip, yellow pepper and bay leaves. Pour in the stock and bring to the boil. Reduce the heat, cover with a lid and simmer for 20 minutes. Stir the tomato purée with a little of the stock, then add to the pan with the chopped tomatoes.

Meanwhile, make the dumplings. Place all the dumpling ingredients except the water in a bowl and stir to mix, then add enough water to bring the ingredients together. Shape into small balls and reserve.

When the vegetables and turkey are tender, add seasoning to taste. Drop the dumplings into the simmering stock and cook for 2–3 minutes until firm. Ladle into bowls and serve with crusty bread.

**Cook's Tip:** If liked, add some flavouring to the dumplings. Try chopped dill or parsley or chives, or try dry mustard powder, paprika or finely grated Parmesan cheese.

# Fish ❧ Seafood

From an everyday family lunch to a swanky dinner party, fish and seafood should not be underestimated when it comes to impressing with a delicious soup recipe. For a warming lunch, opt for the Pumpkin & Smoked Haddock Soup, a perfect combination of flavours. If you are looking for a dinner party starter with a twist, or an idea for a special occasion lunch, then the Saffron Mussel Soup is sure to be a winner.

# New England Clam Chowder

## Serves 4

2 tbsp butter
3 bacon rashers, rind removed
and chopped
2 medium onions, peeled
and chopped
2 garlic cloves, peeled and chopped
25 g/1 oz plain flour
300 g can clams
750 ml/1 1/4 pints water
450 g/1 lb potatoes, peeled
and chopped
2 tbsp celery leaves, chopped
1 bay leaf
salt and freshly ground black pepper
parsley sprigs, to garnish

Heat 1 tablespoon of the butter in a large saucepan and, when melted, add the bacon and fry for 2 minutes, or until just cooked. Using a slotted spoon, remove the bacon from the butter and reserve.

Add the onions and garlic to the butter and cook for 5 minutes, or until the onions are beginning to soften. Return the bacon to the pan and sprinkle in the flour. Cook, stirring, for 2 minutes.

Drain the liquid from the clams and reserve the clams, then gradually stir the clam liquid into the pan together with the potatoes. Slowly bring to the boil, stirring until the mixture comes to the boil. Add the celery leaves, the bay leaf and seasoning to taste.

When boiling, reduce the heat, cover with a lid and simmer for 12–15 minutes until the potatoes are tender. Add the clams to the saucepan together with the remaining butter. Heat for a further 5 minutes. Garnish with parsley and serve.

**Cook's Tip:** If the chowder is too thick, add a little milk. Take care not to allow the chowder to boil, otherwise the potatoes will break up too much.

# Manhattan Clam Chowder

### Serves 4

2 tbsp olive oil
4 rashers streaky bacon, chopped
into small pieces
1 medium onion, peeled
and chopped
2 garlic cloves, peeled and crushed
350 g/12 oz potatoes, peeled
and diced
1 celery stalk, trimmed and chopped
2 tbsp tomato purée
900 ml/1½ pints fish stock
300 g can clams, drained and
liquid reserved
2 medium tomatoes, skinned,
deseeded and chopped
225 g/8 oz canned or frozen
sweetcorn kernels, thawed if frozen
salt and freshly ground black pepper
Tabasco sauce, to taste
300 g/11 oz raw shelled
small prawns
1 tbsp snipped chives
bread or crackers, to serve

Heat the oil in a large saucepan, add the bacon and cook, stirring, for 3 minutes. Add the onion, garlic, potatoes and celery and cook for 10 minutes, stirring frequently, or until the vegetables are beginning to soften.

Blend the tomato purée with a little stock and add to the pan with the remaining stock, the reserved clam liquid and the tomatoes. Bring to the boil, reduce the heat and simmer for 10–15 minutes until the vegetables are almost tender.

Add the sweetcorn with seasoning to taste. Add the Tabasco sparingly as it is very hot. Return to a simmer and cook for a further 5 minutes before adding the clams and prawns. Continue to heat for 3–5 minutes, then adjust the seasoning and stir in the chives. Serve with bread or crackers.

**Cook's Tip:** If fresh prawns are unavailable, use thawed shelled frozen prawns. Add at the end of cooking and allow them to heat through for 2–3 minutes.

# Thai Shellfish Soup

## Serves 4-6

350 g/12 oz raw prawns
350 g/12 oz firm white fish, such as
monkfish, cod or haddock
175 g/6 oz small squid rings
1 tbsp lime juice
450 g/1 lb live mussels
400 ml/14 fl oz coconut milk
1 tbsp groundnut oil
2 tbsp Thai red curry paste
1 lemongrass stalk, bruised
3 kaffir lime leaves, finely shredded
2 tbsp Thai fish sauce
salt and freshly ground
black pepper
fresh coriander leaves, to garnish

Peel the prawns. Using a sharp knife, remove the black vein along the back of the prawns. Pat dry with absorbent kitchen paper and reserve. Skin the fish, pat dry and cut into 2.5 cm/1 inch chunks. Place in a bowl with the prawns and the squid rings. Sprinkle with the lime juice. Reserve.

Scrub the mussels, removing their beards and any barnacles. Discard any mussels that are open, damaged or that do not close when tapped. Place in a large saucepan and add 150 ml/¼ pint of the coconut milk.

Cover, bring to the boil, then simmer for 5 minutes, or until the mussels open, shaking the saucepan occasionally. Lift out the mussels, discarding any unopened ones, carefully strain the liquid through a muslin-lined sieve and reserve.

Rinse and dry the saucepan. Heat the groundnut oil, add the curry paste and cook for 1 minute, stirring all the time. Add the lemongrass, lime leaves and fish sauce and pour in both the strained and the remaining coconut milk. Bring the contents of the saucepan to a very gentle simmer.

Add the fish mixture to the saucepan and simmer for 2–3 minutes until just cooked. Stir in the mussels, with or without their shells, as preferred. Season to taste with salt and pepper, then garnish with coriander leaves. Ladle into warmed bowls and serve immediately.

# Lobster Bisque

### Serves 4

1 small cooked lobster
50 g/2 oz butter
1 medium onion, peeled
and chopped
1 leek, trimmed and sliced
1 large carrot, peeled and sliced
150 ml/¼ pint dry white wine
1 litre/1¾ pints water
1 bay leaf
50 g/2 oz long-grain rice
225 g/8 oz fresh ripe tomatoes,
skinned, deseeded and chopped
juice of ½ lemon
salt and freshly ground black pepper
few drops Tabasco sauce, or to taste
4 tbsp single cream
bread, to serve

Cut the lobster into small pieces, removing the meat from the claws. Cut into pieces and rinse lightly to remove any small bits of shell. Heat half the butter in a saucepan, add the lobster meat and shell and fry for 4 minutes, or until the flesh is lightly browned.

Add half the vegetables and the bay leaf and cook, stirring, for 5 minutes, then pour in the wine. Bring to the boil and boil for 1 minute, then add the water. Return to the boil, then reduce the heat, cover with a lid and simmer for 1 hour. Strain, discarding the shell and reserving the meat and stock.

Melt the remaining butter in a large saucepan, add the remaining vegetables and cook, stirring, for 5 minutes, then add the rice and stock. Bring to the boil, then reduce the heat, cover with a lid and simmer for 25 minutes.

Add the tomatoes to the soup with the lobster meat, lemon juice, seasoning and Tabasco to taste. Whizz in a food processor until smooth, then return to a clean saucepan and stir in the cream. Heat for 5 minutes, then serve with bread.

**Cook's Tip:** Many supermarkets sell frozen cooked lobster, which can be used in place of fresh ones.

# Thai Spicy Prawn & Lettuce Noodle Soup

### Serves 4

225 g/8 oz raw tiger prawns
1 tbsp groundnut or vegetable oil
2 garlic cloves, peeled and crushed
1 red chilli, deseeded and
finely chopped
1 tbsp freshly grated root ginger
4 spring onions, trimmed and
finely sliced
1.1 litres/2 pints chicken stock
1 kaffir lime leaf, finely shredded
1 lemongrass stalk, outer leaves
discarded and finely chopped
75 g/3 oz shiitake mushrooms, sliced
125 g/4 oz medium egg
thread noodles
50 g/2 oz lettuce, shredded
75 g/3 oz beansprouts

Peel the prawns, leaving the tail tip on. Cut almost in half down the back of the prawn, discarding any dark veins, and open out. Rinse lightly, then pat dry with absorbent kitchen paper and reserve.

Heat a wok until very hot, then add the oil and, when hot, add the garlic, chilli, ginger and spring onions and stir-fry for 30 seconds. Add the prawns and stir-fry for a further 1 minute.

Add the chicken stock, lime leaf and lemongrass and bring to the boil. Reduce the heat and simmer for 10 minutes, adding the mushrooms after 7–8 minutes.

Meanwhile, cook the noodles in plenty of boiling water according to the packet instructions. Drain well. Add to the soup with the lettuce and beansprouts and return to the boil; simmer for about 30 seconds. Divide the soup between individual bowls and serve immediately.

# Udon Prawn Noodle Soup

## Serves 4

400 g/14 oz wheat udon noodles
125 g/4 oz watercress
2 medium eggs
1 litre/1¾ pints dashi or fish or
vegetable stock
6 tbsp soy sauce
2 tbsp soft light brown sugar or
caster sugar
2 tbsp mirin or rice wine or sake
1 red pepper, deseeded
and chopped
1 green pepper, deseeded
and chopped
4 shiitake mushrooms, sliced
4 frozen shelled prawns, thawed
4–6 spring onions, trimmed and
finely chopped
25 g/1 oz dried ready-to-eat
seaweed
lime wedges, to garnish

Cook the noodles in plenty of water for 4–5 minutes according to the packet instructions until tender, then drain and reserve. Blanch the watercress in boiling water for 1 minute, then drain and reserve. Boil the eggs for 10 minutes, or until hard, then drain, plunge into cold water and leave until cold. Peel and cut in half.

Place the dashi or stock in a large saucepan and add the soy sauce, sugar, mirin and chopped peppers. Bring to the boil, then reduce the heat to a simmer and cook for 5 minutes until the sugar has dissolved.

Add the mushrooms and cook for 30 seconds before adding the prawns. Divide the watercress, spring onions and seaweed between bowls and top with the reserved noodles. Chop the eggs finely, then sprinkle over the noodles and mix lightly together. Pour the soup over the top and serve with lime wedges.

**Cook's Tip:** Both dashi and mirin are Japanese ingredients, which are used extensively in Japanese cuisine. The suggested alternatives will work and are readily available, but will alter the flavour of the finished soup.

# Pumpkin  Smoked Haddock Soup

## Serves 4–6

2 tbsp olive oil
1 medium onion, peeled
and chopped
2 garlic cloves, peeled
and chopped
3 celery stalks, trimmed
and chopped
700 g/1¹/₂ lb pumpkin, peeled,
deseeded and cut into chunks
450 g/1 lb potatoes, peeled and cut
into chunks
750 ml/1¹/₄ pints chicken
stock, heated
125 ml/4 fl oz dry sherry
200 g/7 oz smoked haddock fillet
150 ml/¹/₄ pint milk
freshly ground black pepper
2 tbsp freshly chopped parsley

Heat the oil in a large, heavy-based saucepan and gently cook the onion, garlic and celery for about 10 minutes. This will release the sweetness but not colour the vegetables. Add the pumpkin and potatoes to the saucepan and stir to coat the vegetables with the oil.

Gradually pour in the stock and bring to the boil. Cover, then reduce the heat and simmer for 25 minutes, stirring occasionally. Stir in the dry sherry, then remove the saucepan from the heat and leave to cool for 5–10 minutes.

Blend the mixture in a food processor or blender to form a chunky purée and return to the cleaned saucepan.

Meanwhile, place the fish in a shallow frying pan. Pour in the milk with 3 tablespoons water and bring to almost boiling point. Reduce the heat, cover and simmer for 6 minutes, or until the fish is cooked and flakes easily. Remove from the heat and, using a slotted spoon, remove the fish from the liquid, reserving both liquid and fish.

Discard the skin and any bones from the fish and flake into pieces. Stir the fish liquid into the soup together with the flaked fish. Season with freshly ground black pepper, stir in the parsley and serve immediately.

# Cioppino
# (Italian-American Fish Stew)

### Serves 4

900 g/2 lb assorted seafood, such
as cod, prawns, squid, scallops,
clams and mussels
50 g/2 oz butter
1 large onion, peeled and chopped
2–3 garlic cloves, peeled
and crushed
1 tbsp freshly chopped parsley,
plus extra to garnish
1 tsp freshly chopped basil
1 tsp freshly chopped thyme
1 tsp freshly chopped oregano
2 bay leaves
400 g can chopped tomatoes
300 ml/¹/₂ pint water
150 ml/¹/₄ pint dry white wine
900 ml/1¹/₂ pints fish stock
large cooked prawns, with shells,
heads and tails intact, to garnish
lemon wedges, to serve

Prepare all the seafood. Skin and remove any bones from any white fish and cut into small pieces. Peel any prawns, leaving a few unpeeled ones for the garnish. Clean the squid if necessary and cut into rings, and slice any scallops, reserving the coral roe. Scrub the clams and mussels, discarding any that are open and removing any barnacles on the shells. Place all the seafood in a bowl of cold water and leave in a cold place or the refrigerator.

Melt the butter in a large saucepan, add the onion and garlic and fry for 5 minutes, then add the chopped herbs and cook, stirring, for 1 minute, then add the tomatoes, water, wine and stock. Bring to the boil, then reduce the heat and simmer for 30 minutes.

Add the prepared seafood according to length of cooking time and cook for 3–5 minutes, then remove from the heat, cover with a lid or cloth and leave for 5 minutes. Garnish with a few prawns and chopped parsley and serve with lemon wedges.

Cook's Tip: Vary the seafood used in this Italian recipe according to availability and personal preference – try fresh haddock, monkfish, salmon and crab.

# Sour-&-Spicy Prawn Soup

## Serves 4

50 g/2 oz rice noodles
25 g/1 oz Chinese dried mushrooms
4 spring onions, trimmed
2 small green chillies
3 tbsp freshly chopped coriander
600 ml/1 pint chicken stock
2.5 cm/1 inch piece fresh root
ginger, peeled and grated
2 lemongrass stalks, outer leaves
discarded and finely chopped
4 kaffir lime leaves
12 raw king prawns, peeled with tail
shell left on
2 tbsp Thai fish sauce
2 tbsp lime juice
salt and freshly ground
black pepper

Place the noodles in cold water and leave to soak while preparing the soup. Place the dried mushrooms in a small bowl, cover with almost-boiling water and leave for 20–30 minutes. Drain, strain and reserve the soaking liquor and discard any woody stems from the mushrooms.

Finely shred the spring onions and place into a small bowl. Cover with ice-cold water and refrigerate until required and the spring onions have curled.

Place the green chillies with 2 tablespoons of the chopped coriander in a pestle and mortar and pound to a paste. Reserve.

Pour the stock into a saucepan and bring gently to the boil. Stir in the ginger, lemongrass and lime leaves with the reserved mushrooms and their liquor. Return to the boil.

Drain the noodles, add to the soup with the prawns, Thai fish sauce and lime juice and then stir in the chilli and coriander paste. Bring to the boil, then simmer for 3 minutes. Stir in the remaining chopped coriander and season to taste with salt and pepper. Ladle into warmed bowls, sprinkle with the spring onion curls and serve immediately.

# Cream of Salmon Soup

## Serves 4

1.7 litres/3 pints water
350 g/12 oz potatoes, peeled and cut into chunks
1 large onion, peeled and chopped
salt and freshly ground black pepper
1 bouquet garni
3 fresh dill sprigs, plus extra to garnish
350 g/12 oz fresh salmon fillet
2 tbsp lime juice
300 ml/1/2 pint single cream
sour cream, to garnish
lime slices, to garnish

Place the water, potatoes and onion with seasoning to taste in a medium saucepan and add the bouquet garni and dill sprigs. Bring to the boil, then cover with a lid, reduce the heat and simmer for 10 minutes, or until the potatoes are almost tender.

Remove the skin from the salmon and discard any fine pin bones. Cut into small chunks and add to the pan with the lime juice. Cover with the lid and simmer for 12–15 minutes until the salmon is cooked.

Remove the bouquet garni and leave to cool for a few minutes, then whizz the soup in a food processor until smooth. Return to a clean pan, then slowly stir in the single cream and heat gently until hot.

Adjust the seasoning, then serve in warmed bowls topped with a spoonful of sour cream, slices of lime and a small sprig of dill.

**Cook's Tip:** This soup would be good to serve chilled on a hot summer's day. Make as above, chill for at least 3 hours and add the garnish just before serving.

# Cullen Skink

## Serves 4

25 g/1 oz unsalted butter
1 onion, peeled and chopped
1 fresh bay leaf
25 g/1 oz plain flour
350 g/12 oz new potatoes,
scrubbed and cut into
small pieces
600 ml/1 pint semi-skimmed milk
300 ml/$\frac{1}{2}$ pint water
350 g/12 oz undyed smoked
haddock fillet, skinned
75 g/3 oz sweetcorn kernels
50 g/2 oz garden peas
freshly ground black pepper
$\frac{1}{2}$ tsp freshly grated nutmeg
2–3 tbsp single cream
2 tbsp freshly chopped parsley
crusty bread, to serve

Melt the butter in a large, heavy-based saucepan, add the onion and sauté for 3 minutes, stirring occasionally. Add the bay leaf and stir, then sprinkle in the flour and cook over a low heat for 2 minutes, stirring frequently. Add the potatoes.

Take off the heat and gradually stir in the milk and water. Return to the heat and bring to the boil, stirring. Reduce the heat to a simmer and cook for 10 minutes.

Meanwhile, discard any pin bones from the fish and cut into small pieces. Add to the pan together with the sweetcorn and peas. Cover and cook gently, stirring occasionally, for 10 minutes, or until the vegetables and fish are cooked.

Add pepper and nutmeg to taste, then stir in the cream and heat gently for 1–2 minutes until piping hot. Sprinkle with the parsley and serve with crusty bread.

# Calamari Soup

## Serves 4

350 g/12 oz ready-prepared
calamari
2 tbsp olive oil
1 medium onion, peeled
and chopped
2 garlic cloves, peeled and crushed
1 carrot, peeled and chopped
1 yellow pepper, deseeded
and chopped
1 tbsp thyme sprigs
2 tbsp tomato purée
1. 1 litres/2 pints fish or
vegetable stock
450 g/1 lb ripe fresh tomatoes,
skinned and cut into small slices
salt and freshly ground
black pepper
pinch cayenne pepper

If necessary, cut the calamari into small rings or pieces and rinse lightly. Pat dry with kitchen paper and reserve.

Heat the oil in a saucepan, add the onion, garlic, carrot, pepper and thyme and cook for 5 minutes, or until the onion is beginning to soften. Blend the tomato purée with a little stock, then pour into the pan together with the remaining stock. Bring to the boil, cover with a lid, reduce the heat and simmer for 20 minutes.

Add the tomatoes and seasoning to taste and cook for 10 minutes, or until the tomatoes have begun to collapse. Stir the prepared calamari into the soup and cook for 3 minutes. Adjust the seasoning and add cayenne to taste and continue to cook for a further 5 minutes, or until the calamari is cooked. Serve.

**Cook's Tip:** Take care when cooking any type of calamari, as it cooks very quickly and, if it's overcooked, becomes very tough.

# Chunky Salmon Soup

## Serves 4

450 g/1 lb fresh salmon
2 tbsp olive oil
2 medium onions, peeled
and chopped
3 celery stalks, trimmed
and chopped
225 g/8 oz carrots, peeled
and chopped
300 g/11 oz potatoes, peeled
and diced
2 tbsp plain flour
600 ml/1 pint fish or vegetable stock
225 g/8 oz courgette, peeled,
deseeded and cut into
small pieces
few dill sprigs. plus extra to garnish
4 tbsp lemon juice
300 ml/$^1$/$_2$ pint single cream
salt and freshly ground black pepper

Skin the salmon and remove the skin and any fine pin bones. Cut into small pieces and reserve.

Heat the oil in a large saucepan, add the vegetables and fry, stirring frequently, for 10 minutes, or until the vegetables have begun to soften. Sprinkle in the flour and cook for 2 minutes. Remove from the heat and gradually stir in the stock, then add the courgette, dill sprigs and lemon juice.

Return to the heat and bring to the boil. Reduce the heat, cover with a lid and simmer for 15 minutes, checking once or twice that the liquid is not evaporating too much. If it is, add a little more.

Add the salmon and continue to cook for a further 15–20 minutes until the vegetables and salmon are tender. Once cooked, stir in the cream and add seasoning to taste. Ladle into warmed bowls, garnish with extra dill sprigs and serve.

# Prawn & Chilli Soup

## Serves 4

2 spring onions, trimmed
225 g/8 oz whole raw
tiger prawns
750 ml/1¼ pints fish stock
finely grated zest and juice
of 1 lime
1 tbsp fish sauce
1 red chilli, deseeded
and chopped
1 tbsp soy sauce
1 lemongrass stalk
2 tbsp rice vinegar
4 tbsp freshly
chopped coriander

To make spring onion curls, finely shred the spring onions lengthways. Place in a bowl of ice-cold water and reserve.

Remove the heads and shells from the prawns, leaving the tails intact. Split the prawns almost in two to form a butterfly shape and remove the black thread that runs down the back of each one.

In a large pan, heat the stock with the lime zest and juice, fish sauce, chilli and soy sauce.

Bruise the lemongrass by crushing it along its length with a rolling pin, then add to the stock mixture.

When the stock mixture is boiling, add the prawns and cook until they are pink.

Remove the lemongrass and add the rice vinegar and coriander. Ladle into bowls and garnish with the spring onion curls. Serve immediately.

# Fish Solyanka

## Serves 4

450 g/1 lb fresh salmon fillet
2 tbsp olive oil
2 medium onions, peeled
and chopped
2 garlic cloves, peeled and crushed
1 celery stalk, trimmed and chopped
2 tbsp tomato purée
900 ml/1¹/₂ pints fish or
vegetable stock
1 tbsp butter
2 bay leaves
2 tomatoes, chopped
4 dill pickled cucumbers, chopped
25 g/1 oz black olives, pitted
salt and freshly ground
black pepper
1 tbsp freshly chopped dill
crusty bread, to serve

## To garnish:

sour cream
lemon slices

Discard the skin from the fish and any fine pin bones, then cut into small slices. Rinse lightly and pat dry with kitchen paper. Reserve.

Heat the oil in a large saucepan, add the onions, garlic and celery and fry gently for 5–8 minutes until beginning to soften. Blend the tomato purée with a little stock, then pour into the saucepan together with the remaining stock and the butter. Bring to the boil, stirring, then reduce the heat to a gentle simmer.

Add the bay leaves, cover with a lid and simmer for 15 minutes. Take care that the stock is not evaporating too quickly; if so, reduce the heat a little more.

Add the fish, tomatoes, pickled cucumbers and olives and continue to simmer for a further 5 minutes, or until the fish is tender and just cooked. Add seasoning to taste, then add the chopped dill. Ladle into bowls and garnish with spoonfuls of sour cream and lemon slices. Serve with crusty bread.

**Cook's Tip:** This soup originates in Russia, where they use sturgeon, but this is not readily available in the UK, so salmon is an excellent alternative.

# Mediterranean Chowder

### Serves 6

1 tbsp olive oil
1 tbsp butter
1 large onion, peeled and
finely sliced
4 celery stalks, trimmed and
thinly sliced
2 garlic cloves, peeled and crushed
1 bird's-eye chilli, deseeded and
finely chopped
1 tbsp plain flour
225 g/8 oz potatoes, peeled
and diced
600 ml/1 pint fish or vegetable stock
700 g/1$\frac{1}{2}$ lb whiting or cod fillet, cut
into 2.5 cm/1 inch cubes
2 tbsp freshly chopped parsley
125 g/4 oz large peeled prawns
198 g can sweetcorn, drained
salt and freshly ground
black pepper
150 ml/$\frac{1}{4}$ pint single cream
1 tbsp freshly snipped chives
warm crusty bread, to serve

Heat the oil and butter together in a large saucepan, add the onion, celery and garlic and cook gently for 2–3 minutes until softened. Add the chilli and stir in the flour. Cook, stirring, for a further minute.

Add the potatoes to the saucepan with the stock. Bring to the boil, cover and simmer for 10 minutes. Add the fish cubes to the saucepan with the chopped parsley and cook for a further 5–10 minutes until the fish and potatoes are just tender.

Stir in the peeled prawns and sweetcorn and season to taste with salt and pepper. Pour in the cream and adjust the seasoning if necessary.

Scatter the snipped chives over the top of the chowder. Ladle into six large bowls and serve immediately with plenty of warm crusty bread.

# Saffron Mussel Soup

## Serves 4

¹/₄ tsp saffron strands
150 ml/¹/₄ pint warm water
900 g/2 lb live mussels
2 tbsp olive oil
¹/₂ tsp curry powder
1 medium onion, peeled
and chopped
4 garlic cloves, peeled and chopped
1 celery stalk, trimmed and chopped
1 leek, trimmed and sliced
150 ml/¹/₄ pint dry white wine
1.1 litres/2 pints fish stock
2 bay leaves
salt and freshly ground black pepper
150 ml/¹/₄ pint double cream
freshly chopped chives
fresh chervil sprigs, to garnish

Soak the saffron in the warm water for 15 minutes. Meanwhile, prepare the mussels by discarding any that are open, then removing any barnacles and beards. Scrub the shells and cover with cold water and leave in a cold room or the refrigerator until required.

Heat the oil in a large saucepan, add the curry powder and fry for 30 seconds. Add the onion, garlic, celery and leek and fry for 8–10 minutes until the vegetables are beginning to soften. Pour in the wine and let it bubble for 1 minute.

Add the stock with the saffron and its soaking liquid together with the bay leaves, then bring to the boil, reduce the heat and simmer for 15 minutes. Take care to keep the heat to a simmer, otherwise the stock will boil away.

Add seasoning to taste. Drain the prepared mussels and add to the pan. Cover with a lid and cook for 4–5 minutes until the mussels have opened. Stir in the cream and chives, ladle into warmed bowls, garnish with chervil and serve.

# Thai Hot-&-Sour Prawn Soup

## Serves 4

700 g/1¹/₂ lb large raw prawns
2 tbsp vegetable oil
3–4 lemongrass stalks, outer leaves
discarded and coarsely chopped
2.5 cm/1 inch piece fresh root ginger,
peeled and finely chopped
2–3 garlic cloves, peeled
and crushed
small bunch fresh coriander, leaves
stripped and reserved, stems
finely chopped
¹/₂ tsp freshly ground black pepper
1.8 litres/3¹/₄ pints water
1–2 small red chillies, deseeded and
thinly sliced
1–2 small green chillies, deseeded
and thinly sliced
6 kaffir lime leaves, thinly shredded
4 spring onions, trimmed and
diagonally sliced
1–2 tbsp Thai fish sauce
1–2 tbsp freshly squeezed lime juice

Remove the heads from the prawns by twisting away from the body and reserve. Peel the prawns, leaving the tails on and reserve the shells with the heads. Using a sharp knife, remove the black vein from the back of the prawns. Rinse and dry the prawns and reserve. Rinse and dry the heads and shells.

Heat a wok, add the oil and, when hot, add the prawn heads and shells, the lemongrass, ginger, garlic, coriander stems and black pepper and stir-fry for 2–3 minutes until the prawn heads and shells turn pink and all the ingredients are coloured.

Carefully add the water to the wok and return to the boil, skimming off any scum which rises to the surface. Simmer over a medium heat for 10 minutes, or until slightly reduced. Strain through a fine sieve and return the clear prawn stock to the wok.

Bring the stock back to the boil and add the reserved prawns, chillies, lime leaves and spring onions and simmer for 3 minutes, or until the prawns turn pink. Season with the fish sauce and lime juice. Spoon into warmed soup bowls, dividing the prawns evenly and float a few coriander leaves over the surface.

# Scallop Noodle Soup

### Serves 4

175 g/6 oz rice noodles
1 tbsp sunflower oil
small piece root ginger, peeled and
thinly sliced
1 medium onion, peeled and sliced
1 green chilli, deseeded
and chopped
6 shiitake mushrooms, cleaned
and sliced
1 tsp Thai fish sauce
2 lemongrass stalks, bruised
2 tbsp lime juice
900 ml/1$\frac{1}{2}$ pints fish or
vegetable stock
125 g/4 oz Chinese white cabbage,
outer leaves discarded
125 g/4 oz mangetout
salt and freshly ground black pepper
12 fresh scallops, or use thawed
frozen scallops
25 g/1 oz butter, or oil if preferred

Soak the noodles according to the packet instructions and reserve. Heat the oil in a large saucepan or wok and, when hot, stir-fry the ginger, onion, chilli and mushrooms for 3 minutes. Add the fish sauce, lemongrass and lime juice. Remove the mushrooms and reserve.

Pour in the stock, bring to the boil, then reduce the heat and simmer for 3–5 minutes to allow the flavours to develop. Add the reserved mushrooms and Chinese cabbage and cook for 3 minutes, then add the mangetout with seasoning to taste. Keep the pan on a very gentle simmer.

Meanwhile, discard any black veins around the scallops and keep or remove the orange coral, according to personal preference. Rinse lightly and pat dry with kitchen paper. Heat the butter or oil in a frying pan and cook the scallops on both sides for 2 minutes, or until cooked and lightly golden. Drain on kitchen paper. To serve, ladle the soup into warmed bowls and place three scallops into each bowl.

**Cook's Tip:** If liked, the lemongrass stalks can be removed before serving, but if left in will give more flavour to the soup.

# Bouillabaisse

## Serves 4–6

700 g/1½ lb assorted fish, such as
whiting, mackerel, red mullet,
salmon and king prawns, cleaned
and skinned
few saffron strands
3 tbsp olive oil
2 onions, peeled and sliced
2 celery stalks, trimmed and sliced
225 g/8 oz ripe tomatoes, peeled
and chopped
1 fresh bay leaf
2–3 garlic cloves, peeled
and crushed
1 bouquet garni
sea salt and freshly ground
black pepper
French bread, to serve

Cut the fish into thick pieces, peel the prawns if necessary, and rinse well. Place the saffron strands in a small bowl, cover with warm water and leave to infuse for at least 10 minutes.

Heat the oil in a large, heavy-based saucepan or casserole dish, add the onions and celery and sauté for 5 minutes, stirring occasionally. Add the tomatoes, bay leaf, garlic and bouquet garni and stir until lightly coated with the oil.

Place the firm fish on top of the tomatoes and pour in the saffron-infused water and enough water to just cover. Bring to the boil, reduce the heat, cover with a lid and cook for 8 minutes.

Add the soft-flesh fish and continue to simmer for 5 minutes, or until all the fish are cooked. Season to taste with salt and pepper, remove and discard the bouquet garni and serve with French bread.

# Cream of Potato with Seafood

## Serves 4

2 tbsp olive oil

1 medium onion, peeled and chopped

2 garlic cloves, peeled and chopped

½ celeriac, peeled and chopped

350 g/12 oz potatoes, peeled and chopped

900 ml/1½ pints vegetable or fish stock

2 bay leaves

300 ml/½ pint milk

350 g/12 oz cod fillet or other white fish

1 fresh large prepared crab or 300 g/11 oz canned or frozen crab meat

2 dill sprigs, plus extra to garnish

salt and freshly ground black pepper

Tabasco sauce, to taste

150 ml/¼ pint single cream or crème fraîche

bread or Parmesan crisps, to serve

Heat the oil in a large saucepan, then add the onion, garlic, celeriac and potatoes and cook over a gentle heat, stirring frequently, for 10 minutes, or until the vegetables begin to soften. Pour in the stock and add the bay leaves.

Bring to the boil, cover with a lid, then reduce the heat and simmer for 15 minutes, or until the vegetables are tender. Remove from the heat and cool slightly, discarding the bay leaves. Whizz in a food processor until smooth and return the soup to the cleaned pan together with the milk.

Skin the cod and discard any bones, then cut into small pieces. Make sure that the crab meat has been removed from the claws and cut a few pieces into small chunks and reserve. If using canned or frozen crab meat, ensure the canned crab is thoroughly drained or the frozen crab meat is thawed.

Heat the soup to simmering point, then add the dill sprigs and prepared cod and crab. Add seasoning and Tabasco to taste and simmer gently for 10–12 minutes until the soup is hot and the fish cooked. Stir in the cream or crème fraîche, then heat for 2 minutes. Serve garnished with the reserved crab, extra dill sprigs and Parmesan crisps.

**Cook's Tip:** Other seafood can be used in this delicious soup. Try monkfish with scallops and raw large prawns or a combination of both smoked and fresh cod fillet.

# Clam Soup

## Serves 4

900 g/2 lb fresh clams
salt and freshly ground black pepper
bread, to serve

### For the stock:
2 tbsp olive oil
2 garlic cloves, peeled and chopped
1 medium onion, peeled and chopped
1 celery stalk, trimmed and chopped
1 leek, trimmed and sliced
1 tsp thyme leaves
1 bouquet garni
few parsley sprigs
1.1 litres/2 pints water

### For the soup:
1 tbsp olive oil
1 medium onion, peeled and chopped
3 garlic cloves, peeled and chopped
1 celery stalk, trimmed and chopped
150 ml/¼ pint dry white wine
freshly chopped parsley, plus sprigs
to garnish

Discard any clams that are open, then scrub the shells and put into a large bowl. When all the clams have been scrubbed, fill the bowl with cold water and leave in a cool place.

For the stock, heat the oil in a large saucepan, add all the vegetables and cook, stirring, for 5–8 minutes until the onion is beginning to soften. Add the herbs and water with seasoning to taste. Bring to the boil, cover with a lid, reduce the heat and simmer for 1 hour. If the liquid is evaporating too quickly, add more water and reduce the heat. Reserve.

For the soup, heat the oil in a large saucepan, add the onion, garlic and celery and cook for 5 minutes, then add the white wine and bring to the boil. Boil rapidly for 2 minutes, then reduce the heat and add the stock. Add seasoning to taste and cook for 5 minutes.

Drain the prepared clams, add to the soup, then cover with a lid and cook for 5 minutes, stirring occasionally, or until the clams have opened. Stir in the chopped parsley. Garnish with parsley sprigs and serve with bread.

# Tuna Chowder

### Serves 4

2 tsp oil
1 onion, peeled and finely chopped
2 celery stalks, trimmed
and finely sliced
1 tbsp plain flour
600 ml/1 pint milk
200 g can tuna in water
320 g can sweetcorn in
water, drained
2 tsp freshly chopped thyme
salt and freshly ground
black pepper
pinch cayenne pepper
2 tbsp freshly chopped parsley

Heat the oil in a large, heavy-based saucepan. Add the onion and celery and cook gently for about 5 minutes, stirring from time to time until, the onion is softened.

Stir in the flour and cook for about 1 minute to thicken.

Draw the pan off the heat and gradually pour in the milk, stirring throughout.

Add the tuna and its liquid, the drained sweetcorn and the thyme.

Mix gently, then bring to the boil. Cover and simmer for 5 minutes.

Remove the pan from the heat and season to taste with salt and pepper.

Sprinkle the chowder with the cayenne pepper and chopped parsley. Divide into soup bowls and serve immediately.

# Shrimp ❦ Bacon Chowder

## Serves 4

4 whole corn-on-the-cobs
225 g/8 oz back bacon
25 g/1 oz butter
2 medium onions, peeled
and chopped
3 garlic cloves, peeled
and chopped
1 red pepper, finely chopped
350 g/12 oz potatoes, peeled
and diced
2 tbsp plain flour
900 ml/1$\frac{1}{2}$ pints chicken stock
300 ml/$\frac{1}{2}$ pint beer, or extra stock
350 g/12 oz peeled frozen
prawns, thawed
salt and freshly ground
black pepper
$\frac{1}{2}$–1 tsp cayenne pepper,
or to taste
6 spring onions, trimmed
and chopped

Discard the silky threads from the corn cobs and cut away the corn kernels. Reserve. Discard the rind from the bacon and chop.

Heat the butter in a large saucepan, add the bacon, onions, garlic and red pepper and fry for 5 minutes, or until the onion is beginning to soften. Add the diced potatoes and stir until lightly coated in the butter. Sprinkle in the flour and cook for 2 minutes, stirring.

Pour in the stock and half the beer, if using, then bring to the boil, reduce the heat, cover with a lid and simmer for 10 minutes. Add the sweetcorn kernels with the remaining beer, if using, or more stock, and the prawns. Season to taste and add the cayenne. Continue to cook for 5–8 minutes until the potato is cooked. Ladle into bowls and garnish with the chopped spring onions.

**Cook's Tip:** If liked, rashers of smoked bacon can be used instead of back bacon.

# Sweetcorn & Crab Soup

## Serves 4

450 g/1 lb fresh corn-on-the-cob
1.3 litres/2$^1$/$_4$ pints chicken stock
2–3 spring onions, trimmed and finely chopped
1 cm/$^1$/$_2$ inch piece fresh root ginger, peeled and finely chopped
1 tbsp dry sherry or Chinese rice wine
2–3 tsp soy sauce
1 tsp soft light brown sugar
salt and freshly ground black pepper
2 tsp cornflour
225 g/8 oz white crab meat, fresh or canned
1 medium egg white
1 tsp sesame oil
1–2 tbsp freshly chopped coriander

Wash and dry the corns cobs. Using a sharp knife and holding the corn cobs at an angle to the chopping board, cut down along the cobs to remove the kernels, then scrape the cobs to remove any excess milky residue. Put the kernels and the milky residue into a large wok.

Add the chicken stock to the wok and place over a high heat. Bring to the boil, stirring and pressing some of the kernels against the side of the wok to squeeze out the starch to help thicken the soup. Simmer for 15 minutes, stirring occasionally.

Add the spring onions, ginger, sherry or Chinese rice wine, soy sauce and brown sugar to the wok and season to taste with salt and pepper. Simmer for a further 5 minutes, stirring occasionally. Blend the cornflour with 1 tablespoon cold water to form a smooth paste and whisk into the soup. Return to the boil, then simmer over a medium heat until thickened.

Add the crab meat, stirring until blended. Beat the egg white with the sesame oil and stir into the soup in a slow, steady stream, stirring continuously. Stir in the chopped coriander and serve immediately.

# Oyster Soup

## Serves 4

36 live oysters, opened and
juice reserved
25 g/1 oz butter
2 shallots, peeled and chopped
1 small fennel bulb, trimmed
and chopped
300 ml/$\frac{1}{2}$ pint white wine
900 ml/1$\frac{1}{2}$ pints fish stock
2 bay leaves
salt and freshly ground
black pepper
$\frac{1}{4}$ tsp cayenne pepper, or to taste
2 tbsp lemon juice
150 ml/$\frac{1}{4}$ pint double cream
spring onion strips and lemon zest
strands, to garnish
brown bread, to serve

Keep the oyster meat and liquid in a cool place. Heat the butter in a saucepan, add the shallots and fennel and cook, stirring gently, for 5–8 minutes until the shallots and fennel are beginning to soften.

Add the white wine and bring to the boil. Boil for 5 minutes, then reduce the heat to a simmer. Pour in the stock, the reserved oyster liquid and the bay leaves.

Keep 12 of the reserved oysters and add the rest to the stock with a little seasoning, the cayenne pepper and lemon juice, then return to a gentle simmer for 5 minutes.

Pass the soup through a sieve and return to a clean saucepan. Stir in the cream. Adjust the seasoning and add the reserved 12 oysters, breaking them up with a wooden spoon. Ladle into warmed bowls, garnish with spring onion strips and lemon zest strands and serve with brown bread.

# Vegetables

With their range of flavours and healthy credentials, vegetables are ideally suited to use in soups. There are so many different ways they can be cooked and flavoured that you will have trouble choosing which vegetable soup to cook next! You are sure to enjoy Pea & Mint Soup – an excellent way to make the most of seasonal vegetables in abundance, whilst Artichoke Soup with Croutons is perfect for something a little different.

# French Onion Soup

### Serves 4

50 g/2 oz butter
450 g/1 lb onions, peeled and very
thinly sliced
2 garlic cloves, peeled and crushed
1 tsp soft brown sugar
1 tbsp freshly chopped thyme
2 bay leaves
900 ml/1¹/₂ pints vegetable stock
5 tbsp dry sherry
salt and freshly ground black pepper

### For the cheese bread:

1 fresh baguette
2 garlic cloves, peeled and crushed
50 g/2 oz finely grated
Gruyère cheese
2 tsp freshly chopped thyme
or parsley

Heat the butter in a heavy-based saucepan until melted. Add the onions and garlic and cook very gently for 20 minutes, stirring frequently, or until the onions are very tender and turning brown. Add the sugar and continue to cook for 5 minutes, or until the onions are caramelised.

Add the thyme and bay leaves to the onions, then pour in the stock. Bring to the boil, then reduce the heat, cover with a lid and simmer gently for 10 minutes. Add the sherry with seasoning to taste, then discard the bay leaves.

While the soup is cooking, prepare the toast. Preheat the grill. Cut the baguette into slices and toast each slice lightly. Sprinkle the crushed garlic over the slices. Sprinkle the toast with the cheese and cook under the hot grill for 2–3 minutes until the cheese is golden and bubbly.

Ladle the soup into warmed bowls and top with one or two slices of the cheese toast. Sprinkle with the thyme and serve.

**Cook's Tip:** Adding the sugar to the onions while caramelising helps to speed up the process. However, take care, as the onions can easily burn during the process.

# Borscht

1 medium onion
450 g/1 lb raw beetroot
1.1 litres/2 pints vegetable stock
2 tbsp lemon juice
4 tbsp sherry
salt and freshly ground
black pepper

## To garnish:
4 tbsp sour cream
fresh chives, snipped
croutons

Peel the onion, chop finely and place in a large saucepan.

Peel the beetroot if preferred, then grate coarsely. Add the grated beetroot to the large saucepan.

Pour in the stock, bring to the boil and simmer, uncovered, for 40 minutes. Remove from the heat and allow it to cool slightly before straining into a clean saucepan. Stir in the lemon juice and sherry and season with salt and pepper.

Pour into four soup bowls and add 1 tablespoon sour cream to each. Sprinkle with snipped chives and a few croutons. This soup can also be served chilled.

# Lentil Soup with Rosemary

## Serves 4

2 tbsp olive oil
2 garlic cloves, peeled and crushed
1 medium onion, peeled and
finely chopped
2 large carrots, peeled and thinly
sliced or chopped
3 celery stalks, trimmed and
thinly sliced
350 g/12 oz potatoes, peeled
and chopped
175 g/6 oz red split lentils
1.1 litres/2 pints vegetable stock
2 rosemary sprigs, plus extra
to garnish
200 ml/7 fl oz milk
salt and freshly ground black pepper

Heat the oil in a large, heavy-based saucepan, add the garlic, onion and carrots and cook for 5–8 minutes until the onion has started to soften. Add the celery with the potatoes and cook for a further 5 minutes, stirring occasionally to prevent the vegetables sticking to the bottom of the pan.

Add the lentils with the stock and rosemary sprigs. Bring to the boil, then reduce the heat and cover with a lid. Cook for 20–25 minutes until the vegetables and lentils are tender.

Discard the rosemary, then leave to cool for 5 minutes before whizzing in a food processor with 150 ml/$\frac{1}{4}$ pint of the milk until smooth. Return to a clean pan, adding the remaining milk if it's too thick. Season to taste, then reheat until piping hot. Garnish with fresh rosemary and serve.

**Cook's Tips:** If liked, a little chopped bacon can be used. Simply fry for 2 minutes, then add with the vegetables.

There are many types of lentils available, so take care when buying to check the packet instructions, as some need overnight soaking and some a longer time to cook.

# Rich Tomato Soup with Roasted Red Peppers

### Serves 4

2 tsp light olive oil
700 g/1½ lb red peppers, halved and deseeded
450 g/1 lb ripe plum tomatoes, halved
2 onions, unpeeled and quartered
4 garlic cloves, unpeeled
600 ml/1 pint chicken stock
salt and freshly ground black pepper
4 tbsp sour cream
1 tbsp freshly shredded basil

Preheat the oven to 200°C/400°F/Gas Mark 6. Lightly oil a roasting tin with 1 teaspoon of the olive oil. Place the peppers and tomatoes cut-side down in the roasting tin with the onion quarters and the garlic cloves. Spoon over the remaining oil.

Roast in the preheated oven for 30 minutes, or until the skins on the peppers have started to blacken and blister. Allow the vegetables to cool for about 10 minutes, then remove the skins, stalks and seeds from the peppers. Peel away the skins from the tomatoes and onions and squeeze out the garlic.

Place the cooked vegetables into a blender or food processor and blend until smooth. Add the stock and blend again to form a smooth purée. Pour the puréed soup through a sieve, if a smooth soup is preferred, then pour into a saucepan. Bring to the boil, simmer gently for 2–3 minutes, and season to taste with salt and pepper. Serve hot with a swirl of sour cream and a sprinkling of shredded basil on the top.

# Miso Soup

## Serves 4

2.5 cm/1 inch piece
wakame seaweed
15 g/<sup>1</sup>/2 oz instant dashi, or use
3 tbsp good vegetable stock
1 litre/1<sup>3</sup>/4 pints boiling water
2 tbsp miso paste
1 tbsp mirin or rice wine
1 tbsp soy sauce
4 fresh asparagus spears,
trimmed and diagonally sliced
125 g/4 oz fresh or frozen peas,
thawed if frozen
200 g/7 oz silken tofu, drained
and diced
6 spring onions, trimmed and
thinly sliced

Soak the seaweed in a bowl of almost-boiling water for 10 minutes, or until softened. Drain and reserve.

Blend the dashi or vegetable stock in a wok or large saucepan with the boiling water and stir well.

Place the miso paste into a small bowl and slowly whisk in some dashi or stock. Continue until a smooth, creamy consistency is formed, then whisk the mixture into the wok or saucepan, whisking throughout.

Stir in the mirin and soy sauce, then add the asparagus and peas and simmer for 5 minutes.

Add the tofu to the wok or saucepan together with the spring onions and seaweed and simmer for a further 5 minutes, then serve.

**Cook's Tip:** If intending to cook many Japanese dishes, it would be a good idea to invest in some seasonings and pots and pans that are suited to this cuisine, as they are different to Western ones.

# Rice ❧ Tomato Soup

## Serves 4

150 g/5 oz easy-cook basmati rice
400 g can chopped tomatoes
2 garlic cloves, peeled
and crushed
grated zest of $1/2$ lime
2 tbsp extra virgin olive oil
1 tsp sugar
salt and freshly ground black pepper
300 ml/$1/2$ pint vegetable
stock or water, heated

## For the croutons:

2 tbsp prepared pesto sauce
2 tbsp olive oil
6 thin slices ciabatta bread,
cut into 1 cm/$1/2$ inch cubes

Preheat the oven to 220°C/425°F/Gas Mark 7. Rinse and drain the basmati rice. Place the canned tomatoes with their juice in a large, heavy-based saucepan with the garlic, lime, oil and sugar. Season to taste with salt and pepper. Bring to the boil, then reduce the heat, cover and simmer for 10 minutes.

Add the heated vegetable stock or water and the rice, then cook, uncovered, for a further 15–20 minutes until the rice is tender. If the soup is too thick, add a little more water. Reserve and keep warm, if the croutons are not ready.

Meanwhile, to make the croutons, mix the pesto and olive oil in a large bowl. Add the bread cubes and toss until they are coated completely with the mixture. Spread on a baking sheet and bake in the preheated oven for 10–15 minutes until golden and crisp, turning them over halfway through cooking. Serve the soup immediately, sprinkled with the warm croutons.

# Squash Soup

## Serves 4

900 g/2 lb squash, such
as butternut
3 tbsp olive oil
2 medium onions, peeled
and chopped
2 garlic cloves, peeled
and chopped
2–3 fresh rosemary sprigs, plus
extra to garnish
1.1 litres/2 pints vegetable
stock, heated
2 tbsp lemon juice
salt and freshly ground
black pepper
150 ml/¼ pint milk (optional)
paprika, to garnish

Preheat the oven to 180°C/350°F/Gas Mark 4, 10 minutes before cooking. Peel the squash and discard the seeds, then cut into chunks. Place in a roasting tin, pour over the oil and stir, ensuring that the squash is well coated in the oil.

Roast the squash in the oven for 20 minutes. Add the onions, garlic and rosemary sprigs and stir all the vegetables. Return to the oven and cook for a further 20 minutes, or until the vegetables are tender. Remove from the oven and discard the rosemary sprigs. Leave to cool for 3 minutes.

Put the vegetables in a food processor together with the warm stock and whizz until smooth. Pour into a large saucepan and add the lemon juice and seasoning to taste. Heat gently and stir in the milk if a thinner soup is preferred. Serve garnished with fresh rosemary and paprika.

**Cook's Tip:** Other squash can be used if preferred, or a mixture of squashes. Remember, some squashes are more watery than others so it is better to use the firmer varieties.

# Rocket & Potato Soup with Garlic Croutons

## Serves 4

700 g/1½ lb baby new potatoes
1.1 litres/2 pints chicken or
vegetable stock
50 g/2 oz rocket leaves
125 g/4 oz thick sliced white bread
50 g/2 oz unsalted butter
1 tsp groundnut oil
2–4 garlic cloves, peeled
and chopped
125 g/4 oz stale ciabatta bread,
crusts removed
4 tbsp olive oil
salt and freshly ground
black pepper
2 tbsp Parmesan cheese,
finely grated

Place the potatoes in a large saucepan, cover with the stock and simmer gently for 10 minutes. Add the rocket leaves and simmer for a further 5–10 minutes until the potatoes are soft and the rocket has wilted.

Meanwhile, make the croutons. Cut the thick sliced white bread into small cubes and reserve. Heat the butter and groundnut oil in a small frying pan and cook the garlic for 1 minute, stirring well. Remove the garlic. Add the bread cubes to the butter and oil mixture in the frying pan and sauté, stirring continuously, until they are golden brown. Drain the croutons on absorbent kitchen paper and reserve.

Cut the ciabatta bread into small dice and stir into the soup. Cover the saucepan and leave to stand for 10 minutes, or until the bread has absorbed a lot of the liquid.

Stir in the olive oil, season to taste with salt and pepper and serve at once with a few of the garlic croutons scattered over the top and a little grated Parmesan cheese.

# Gazpacho

## Serves 4-6

700 g/1¹/₂ lb ripe tomatoes
1 Spanish onion, peeled and
finely chopped
2 garlic cloves, peeled and crushed
1 green pepper, finely chopped
1 yellow pepper, finely chopped
1 red pepper, finely chopped
¹/₂ cucumber, peeled, deseeded
and finely chopped
4 tbsp lemon juice
2 tbsp white wine vinegar
2–3 tbsp extra virgin olive oil
300 ml/¹/₂ pint tomato juice
salt and freshly ground
black pepper
parsley sprigs, to serve

Make a cross at the top of each tomato and place in a large bowl. Cover with boiling water and leave for at least 2 minutes before skinning. Cut into quarters and discard the seeds and cores. Chop finely and put in a bowl.

Add the onion, garlic and peppers to the tomatoes together with the cucumber.

Blend the lemon juice with the vinegar and olive oil, then pour into the tomato mixture together with the tomato juice and seasoning to taste. Stir, then cover and leave to chill in the refrigerator for at least 30 minutes. Stir before serving, garnished with parsley sprigs.

**Cook's Tip:** If liked, reserve a small amount of the chopped onion, cucumber and peppers in small bowls with some ice and fresh bread croutons and serve alongside the soup so diners can help themselves.

# Mushroom ❧ Sherry Soup

### Serves 4

4 slices day-old white bread
zest of ½ lemon
1 tbsp lemon juice
salt and freshly ground
black pepper
125 g/4 oz assorted wild
mushrooms, lightly rinsed
125 g/4 oz baby button
mushrooms, wiped
2 tsp olive oil
1 garlic clove, peeled
and crushed
6 spring onions, trimmed
and diagonally sliced
600 ml/1 pint chicken stock
4 tbsp dry sherry
1 tbsp freshly snipped chives,
to garnish

Preheat the oven to 180°C/350°F/Gas Mark 4. Remove the crusts from the bread and cut the bread into small cubes.

In a large bowl, toss the cubes of bread with the lemon zest and juice, 2 tablespoons water and plenty of freshly ground black pepper.

Spread the bread cubes onto a lightly oiled, large baking tray and bake for 20 minutes until golden and crisp.

If the wild mushrooms are small, leave some whole. Otherwise, thinly slice all the mushrooms and reserve.

Heat the oil in a saucepan. Add the garlic and spring onions and cook for 1–2 minutes.

Add the mushrooms and cook for 3–4 minutes until they start to soften. Add the chicken stock and stir to mix. Bring to the boil, then reduce the heat to a gentle simmer. Cover and cook for 10 minutes.

Stir in the sherry and season to taste with a little salt and pepper. Pour into warmed bowls, sprinkle over the chives and serve immediately with the lemon croutons.

# Asparagus Soup

## Serves 4

300 g/11 oz fresh asparagus
50 g/2 oz butter
2 medium onions, peeled
and chopped
2 tbsp plain white flour
450 ml/³/₄ pint vegetable
stock, heated
salt and freshly ground black
or white pepper
¹/₄ tsp freshly grated nutmeg
(optional)
300 ml/¹/₂ pint milk
150 ml/¹/₄ pint single cream (optional)
parsley sprigs, to garnish

Trim the woody part off the asparagus spears and, using a vegetable peeler, peel down the sides of each spear. Discard. Cut off the tips and reserve and chop the remainder of the asparagus.

Half-fill a frying pan with water and bring to the boil. Reduce the heat to a simmer, add the asparagus tips and cook for 2–3 minutes until tender. Using a slotted spoon, remove the tips and reserve.

Melt the butter in a large saucepan, add the chopped asparagus and onions and cook for 5–8 minutes until beginning to soften. Remove from the heat and sprinkle in the flour, then return to the heat and cook for 2 minutes, gradually stirring in half the stock with seasoning to taste.

Bring to the boil, reduce the heat, cover with a lid and simmer for 20–25 minutes, gradually adding the remaining stock. When all the stock has been added and the asparagus is tender, remove from the heat and leave to cool.

Whizz the asparagus and stock in a food processor until smooth, then return to the pan and add the nutmeg, if using. Stir in the milk and reserved asparagus tips and heat until hot. Add the cream, if liked, heat for 1–2 minutes, then ladle into bowls, garnish with parsley and serve.

# Bread ❧ Tomato Soup

## Serves 4

900 g/2 lb very ripe tomatoes
4 tbsp olive oil
1 onion, peeled and finely chopped
1 tbsp freshly chopped basil
3 garlic cloves, peeled and crushed
$^{1}/_{4}$ tsp hot chilli powder
salt and freshly ground
black pepper
600 ml/1 pint chicken stock
175 g/6 oz stale white bread
50 g/2 oz cucumber, cut into
small dice
4 whole basil leaves

Make a small cross in the base of each tomato, then place in a bowl and cover with boiling water. Allow to stand for 2 minutes, or until the skins have started to peel away, then drain, remove the skins and seeds and chop into large pieces.

Heat 3 tablespoons of the olive oil in a saucepan and gently cook the onion until softened. Add the skinned tomatoes, chopped basil, garlic and chilli powder and season to taste with salt and pepper. Pour in the stock, cover with a lid, bring to the boil and simmer gently for 15–20 minutes.

Remove the crusts from the bread and break into small pieces. Remove the tomato mixture from the heat and stir in the bread. Cover and leave to stand for 10 minutes, or until the bread has blended with the tomatoes. Season to taste. Serve warm or cold with a swirl of olive oil on the top, garnished with a spoonful of chopped cucumber and basil leaves.

# Pea ❧ Mint Soup

## Serves 4

25 g/1 oz butter
900 g/2 lb fresh young peas, shelled
1 bunch spring onions, about 8,
trimmed and chopped
225 g/8 oz potato, peeled
and chopped
2 tbsp plain flour
900 ml/1½ pints vegetable
stock, heated
2 large mint sprigs, plus extra
to garnish
3 tbsp lemon juice
salt and freshly ground black pepper
sour cream, to garnish

Melt the butter in a large saucepan, add the peas, spring onions and potato and fry for 2 minutes, or until everything is lightly coated in the butter. Sprinkle in the flour and cook for 2 minutes.

Remove from the heat and gradually stir in the warm stock. Return to a medium heat and cook, stirring, until the soup comes to the boil. Add the mint sprigs and lemon juice, then cover with a lid, reduce the heat and simmer for 20 minutes, or until the peas are tender.

Remove from the heat and leave to cool for 5 minutes, then whizz in a food processor until smooth and return to a clean pan. Add seasoning to taste and reheat until hot. Serve garnished with mint and sour cream.

Cook's Tip: Thawed frozen peas will not work so well; increase the potato to double to help the consistency.

# Potato ❧ Fennel Soup

## Serves 4

25 g/1 oz butter
2 large onions, peeled and
thinly sliced
2–3 garlic cloves, peeled
and crushed
1 tsp salt
2 medium potatoes (about
450 g/1 lb in weight), peeled
and diced
1 fennel bulb, trimmed and
finely chopped
$^1/_2$ tsp caraway seeds
1 litre/1$^3/_4$ pints vegetable stock
2 tbsp freshly chopped parsley
freshly ground black pepper
4 tbsp crème fraîche
roughly torn pieces French stick,
to serve

Melt the butter in a large, heavy-based saucepan. Add the onions with the garlic and half the salt, and cook over a medium heat, stirring occasionally, for 7–10 minutes until the onions are very soft and beginning to turn brown.

Add the potatoes, fennel, caraway seeds and the remaining salt. Cook for about 5 minutes, then pour in the vegetable stock. Bring to the boil, partially cover and simmer for 15–20 minutes until the potatoes are tender. Stir in the chopped parsley and add the seasoning to taste.

For a smooth-textured soup, allow to cool slightly, then pour into a food processor or blender and blend until smooth. Reheat the soup gently, then ladle into individual soup bowls. For a chunky soup, omit this blending stage and ladle straight from the saucepan into soup bowls.

Swirl a spoonful of crème fraîche into each bowl and serve immediately with roughly torn pieces of French stick.

# Cream of Broccoli Soup

## Serves 4

700 g/1¹/₂ lb broccoli
25 g/1 oz butter
2 medium onions, peeled and chopped
2 garlic cloves, peeled and chopped
2 celery stalks, trimmed and chopped
2 medium potatoes, about 225 g/8 oz in weight, peeled and chopped
2 tbsp plain flour
900 ml/1¹/₂ pints vegetable stock, heated
300 ml/¹/₂ pint milk
salt and freshly ground black pepper
¹/₄ tsp freshly grated nutmeg
150 ml/¹/₄ pint single cream
parsley sprigs, to garnish

Cut the broccoli into small florets, then peel the thick stalk and discard any tough pieces and chop the remainder. Reserve.

Heat the butter in a large saucepan, add the onions, garlic, celery and broccoli stalks and cook, stirring, for 5 minutes, or until the onions have started to soften. Remove from the heat, then stir in the flour and return to the heat and cook for 2 minutes, stirring.

Remove from the heat and gradually stir in the warm stock. Reserve a few pieces of broccoli, then add the remainder to the saucepan along with the potatoes. Return to the heat and cook, stirring occasionally, until the stock comes to the boil. Reduce the heat, cover with a lid and cook for 15–20 minutes until the vegetables are tender.

Cook the reserved broccoli in lightly salted water for 5–8 minutes until tender, then drain and plunge into cold water. Drain and reserve.

When the vegetables for the soup are tender, leave to cool slightly, then whizz in a food processor, adding the milk to form a soup consistency, then return to a clean saucepan. Add the seasoning together with the nutmeg to taste and stir in the cream. Heat gently until hot, then ladle into warmed bowls, garnish with the reserved blanched broccoli and parsley sprigs serve.

# Hot-&-Sour Mushroom Soup

## Serves 4

4 tbsp sunflower oil
3 garlic cloves, peeled and
finely chopped
3 shallots, peeled and
finely chopped
2 large red chillies, deseeded
and finely chopped
1 tbsp soft brown sugar
large pinch salt
1 litre/1$^{3}$/$_{4}$ pints vegetable stock
250 g/9 oz Thai fragrant rice
5 kaffir lime leaves, torn
2 tbsp soy sauce
grated zest and juice of 1 lemon
250 g/9 oz oyster mushrooms,
wiped and cut into pieces
2 tbsp freshly chopped coriander

## To garnish:

2 green chillies, deseeded and
finely chopped
3 spring onions, trimmed and
finely chopped

Heat the oil in a frying pan, add the garlic and shallots and cook until golden brown and starting to crisp. Remove from the pan and reserve. Add the chillies to the pan and cook until they start to change colour.

Place the garlic, shallots and chillies in a food processor or blender and blend to a smooth purée with 150 ml/$^{1}$/$_{4}$ pint water. Pour the purée back into the pan, add the sugar with a large pinch of salt, then cook gently, stirring, until dark in colour. Take care not to burn the mixture.

Pour the stock into a large saucepan, add the garlic purée, rice, lime leaves, soy sauce and the lemon zest and juice. Bring to the boil, then reduce the heat, cover and simmer gently for about 10 minutes.

Add the mushrooms and simmer for a further 10 minutes, or until the mushrooms and rice are tender. Remove the lime leaves, stir in the chopped coriander and ladle into bowls. Place the chopped green chillies and spring onions in small bowls and serve separately to sprinkle on top of the soup.

# Creamy Courgette Soup

## Serves 4

25 g/1 oz butter
2 garlic cloves, peeled and chopped
1 bunch spring onions, about 8,
trimmed and chopped
350 g/12 oz potatoes, peeled
and chopped
2 tbsp plain flour
900 ml/1½ pints vegetable stock
700 g/1½ lb courgettes, trimmed
and chopped
2 mint or basil sprigs
salt and freshly ground black pepper
150 ml/¼ pint single cream or
crème fraîche, plus extra
for swirling

Melt the butter in a large saucepan, add the garlic and spring onions and cook for 2 minutes, then add the potatoes and cook for a further 5 minutes, stirring frequently. Add the flour and cook for a further 2 minutes.

Remove the pan from the heat and gradually stir in the stock. Return to the heat and bring to the boil. Add the courgettes with the herbs and seasoning to taste and cover with a lid. Reduce the heat and simmer for 15–20 minutes until tender.

When the vegetables are tender, whizz in a food processor until smooth, then return to a clean saucepan and add the cream or crème fraîche. Heat gently, then adjust the seasoning to taste and ladle into warmed bowls. Swirl with cream or crème fraîche and serve.

**Cook's Tip:** Use young, tender courgettes for this soup rather than older ones, which may have lost their flavour.

# Cream of Pumpkin Soup

### Serves 4

900 g/2 lb pumpkin flesh (after
peeling and discarding the seeds)
4 tbsp olive oil
1 large onion, peeled
1 leek, trimmed
1 carrot, peeled
2 celery stalks
4 garlic cloves, peeled and crushed
1.7 litres/3 pints water
salt and freshly ground
black pepper
$^1/_4$ tsp freshly grated nutmeg
150 ml/$^1/_4$ pint single cream
$^1/_4$ tsp cayenne pepper
warm herby bread, to serve

Cut the skinned and deseeded pumpkin flesh into 2.5 cm/1 inch cubes. Heat the olive oil in a large saucepan and cook the pumpkin for 2–3 minutes, coating it completely with oil. Chop the onion and leek finely and cut the carrot and celery into small dice.

Add the vegetables to the saucepan with the garlic and cook, stirring, for 5 minutes, or until they have begun to soften. Cover the vegetables with the water and bring to the boil. Season with plenty of salt and pepper and the nutmeg, cover and simmer for 15–20 minutes until all of the vegetables are tender.

When the vegetables are tender, remove from the heat, cool slightly, then pour into a food processor or blender. Liquidise to form a smooth purée, then pass through a sieve into a clean saucepan.

Adjust the seasoning to taste and add all but 2 tablespoons of the cream and enough water to obtain the correct consistency. Bring the soup to boiling point, add the cayenne pepper and serve immediately, swirled with cream and warm herby bread.

# Cauliflower ❧ Potato Soup

## Serves 4–6

1 firm medium cauliflower
25 g/1 oz butter
2 medium onions, peeled
and chopped
2 garlic cloves, peeled and chopped
3 tbsp plain flour
900 ml/1½ pints vegetable stock
350 g/12 oz potatoes, peeled
and chopped
3 large parsley sprigs, plus extra
to garnish
salt and freshly ground black pepper
150 ml/¼ pint single cream or
crème fraîche
toast, to serve

Remove the tough outer leaves from the cauliflower and discard. Divide the cauliflower and any remaining leaves and stalks into small pieces.

Heat the butter in a large saucepan, add the onions and garlic and cook for 5 minutes, stirring frequently, until the onion is beginning to soften. Remove from the heat, stir in the flour, then return to the heat and cook for a further 2 minutes, stirring frequently. Remove the pan from the heat, gradually stir in the stock and return to the heat.

Add the cauliflower and parsley. Bring to the boil, cover with a lid and reduce the heat and simmer for 15–20 minutes until the vegetables are tender. Leave to cool, then discard the parsley sprigs. If liked, remove a small amount of the cooked potato and reserve.

Whizz the soup in a food processor until smooth, then return to a clean saucepan. Add seasoning to taste and stir in the cream with the reserved cooked potato, if using. Heat gently until hot, then garnish with parsley and a sprinkle of ground black pepper and serve with toast.

# Lettuce Soup

## Serves 4

2 iceberg lettuces, quartered, with
hard core removed
1 tbsp olive oil
50 g/2 oz butter
125 g/4 oz spring onions, trimmed
and chopped
1 tbsp freshly chopped parsley
1 tbsp plain flour
600 ml/1 pint chicken stock
salt and freshly ground
black pepper
150 ml/$^1$/$_4$ pint single cream
$^1$/$_4$ tsp cayenne pepper, to taste
thick slices stale ciabatta bread
parsley sprig, to garnish

Bring a large saucepan of water to the boil and blanch the lettuce
leaves for 3 minutes. Drain and dry thoroughly on absorbent kitchen
paper, then shred with a sharp knife.

Heat the oil and butter in a clean saucepan and add the lettuce,
spring onions and parsley and cook together for 3–4 minutes
until very soft.

Stir in the flour and cook for 1 minute, then gradually pour in the
stock, stirring throughout. Bring to the boil and season to taste
with salt and pepper. Reduce the heat, cover with a lid and simmer
gently for 10–15 minutes until soft.

Allow the soup to cool slightly, then either sieve or purée in a blender.
Alternatively, leave the soup chunky. Stir in the cream, add more
seasoning to taste, if liked, then add the cayenne pepper.

Arrange the slices of ciabatta bread in a large soup dish or in
individual bowls and pour the soup over the bread. Garnish with
sprigs of parsley and serve immediately.

# Cream of Sweet Potato Soup

## Serves 4

2 tbsp olive oil
700 g/1¹/₂ lb sweet potato, peeled
and cut into chunks
1 large onion, peeled and chopped
2–3 garlic cloves, peeled
and chopped
2 carrots, about 125 g/4 oz, peeled
and chopped
3 tbsp plain flour
1 tsp curry powder, or to taste
1 tbsp freshly chopped thyme or
1 tsp dried thyme
1 tbsp freshly chopped basil
900 ml/1¹/₂ pints vegetable stock
salt and freshly ground
black pepper
150 ml/¹/₄ pint single cream or
creme fraîche
parsley sprigs, to garnish
crusty bread, to serve

Heat the oil in a large saucepan, add the sweet potato, onion, garlic and carrots and gently fry for 5 minutes, stirring occasionally to stop the vegetables sticking to the base of the saucepan.

Add the flour and curry powder and cook for a further 2 minutes, then add the herbs, stock and seasoning to taste. Bring to the boil, reduce the heat and simmer for 20 minutes, or until the vegetables are tender. Remove from the heat and leave to cool for 5 minutes.

Whizz the soup in a food processor until smooth, then return to a clean saucepan. Adjust the seasoning and stir in the cream or crème fraîche. Heat gently until hot, then garnish with parsley and serve with crusty bread.

**Cook's Tip:** For a change, add some thawed frozen peas to the finished soup, heating for 3–4 minutes before serving.

# Italian Bean Soup

## Serves 4

2 tsp olive oil
1 leek, washed and chopped
1 garlic clove, peeled and crushed
2 tsp dried oregano
75 g/3 oz green beans, trimmed and
cut into bite-size pieces
410 g can cannellini beans, drained
and rinsed
75 g/3 oz small pasta shapes
1 litre/1³/₄ pints vegetable stock
8 cherry tomatoes
salt and freshly ground
black pepper
3 tbsp freshly shredded basil

Heat the oil in a large saucepan. Add the leek, garlic and oregano and cook gently for 5 minutes, stirring occasionally.

Stir in the green beans and the cannellini beans. Sprinkle in the pasta and pour in the stock.

Bring the stock mixture to the boil, then reduce the heat to a simmer. Cook for 12–15 minutes until the vegetables are tender and the pasta is cooked to *al dente*. Stir occasionally.

In a heavy-based frying pan, dry-fry the tomatoes over a high heat until they soften and the skins begin to blacken.

Gently crush the tomatoes in the pan with the back of a spoon and add to the soup.

Season to taste with salt and pepper. Stir in the shredded basil and serve immediately.

# Spicy Tomato Noodle Soup

### Serves 4

700 g/1½ lb ripe tomatoes
125 g/4 oz fine dried noodles
2 tbsp sunflower oil
1 large onion, peeled and chopped
2 large garlic cloves, peeled
and chopped
2 celery stalks, trimmed and sliced
1–2 red chillies, deseeded
and chopped
1 whole star anise
4 green cardamom pods, bruised
and seeds removed
1 tbsp tomato purée
600 ml/1 pint vegetable stock
salt and freshly ground
black pepper
fresh coriander sprigs, to garnish
crusty bread, to serve

Make a cross at the top of each tomato and place in a large, heatproof bowl. Cover the tomatoes with boiling water and leave for 2 minutes. Using a slotted spoon, remove the tomatoes and skin them, then cut into quarters and discard the cores. Chop the tomatoes and reserve.

Cover the noodles with almost-boiling water and leave for about 5 minutes to soften, then drain and reserve.

Heat the oil in a large saucepan, add the onion, garlic and celery and cook for 5 minutes, or until the onion is beginning to soften. Add the chopped chillies with the star anise and cardamom seeds and cook for 1 minute before adding the tomatoes.

Blend the tomato purée with the stock, then stir into the pan. Bring to the boil, then reduce the heat, cover with a lid and simmer for 15 minutes, or until the tomatoes have fully collapsed. Add seasoning to taste. Leave to cool.

Discard the star anise, then whizz the soup in a food processor until smooth. Return to a clean saucepan. Drain the noodles, reserving a few for the garnish, and place in warmed bowls. Ladle the hot soup over, garnish with the reserved noodles and the coriander and serve with crusty bread.

**Cook's Tip:** If you prefer to keep the soup chunky, do not food process it.

# Potato, Leek & Rosemary Soup

## Serves 4

50 g/2 oz butter
450 g/1 lb leeks, trimmed
and finely sliced
700 g/1½ lb potatoes, peeled and
roughly chopped
900 ml/1½ pints vegetable stock
4 fresh rosemary sprigs
450 ml/¾ pint full-cream milk
2 tbsp freshly chopped parsley
2 tbsp crème fraîche
salt and freshly ground
black pepper
wholemeal rolls, to serve

Melt the butter in a large saucepan, add the leeks and cook gently for 5 minutes, stirring frequently. Remove 1 tablespoon of the cooked leeks and reserve for garnishing.

Add the potatoes, vegetable stock, rosemary sprigs and milk. Bring to the boil, then reduce the heat, cover with a lid and simmer gently for 20–25 minutes until the vegetables are tender.

Cool for 10 minutes. Discard the rosemary, then pour into a food processor or blender and blend well to form a smooth-textured soup.

Return the soup to the cleaned saucepan and stir in the chopped parsley and crème fraîche. Season to taste with salt and pepper. If the soup is too thick, stir in a little more milk or water. Reheat gently without boiling, then ladle into warmed soup bowls. Garnish the soup with the reserved leeks and serve immediately with wholemeal rolls.

# Corn Chowder

## Serves 4

25 g/1 oz butter
2 medium onions, peeled
and chopped
2 garlic cloves, peeled
and chopped
1 large green pepper,
finely chopped
350 g/12 oz potatoes, peeled
and diced
2 tbsp plain flour
900 ml/11¹/₂ pints vegetable stock
125 g/4 oz sweetcorn kernels
salt and freshly ground
black pepper
roughly chopped parsley, to garnish
crusty bread, to serve

Heat the butter in a large saucepan, add the onions, garlic and pepper and fry for 5 minutes, or until the onion is beginning to soften. Add the diced potatoes and stir until lightly coated in the butter. Sprinkle in the flour and cook for 2 minutes, stirring.

Pour in the stock and bring to the boil, reduce the heat, cover with a lid and simmer for 10 minutes.

Add the sweetcorn and seasoning to taste, then cook for a further 5–8 minutes until the potato is cooked. Adjust the seasoning, garnish with parsley and serve with crusty bread.

**Cook's Tip:** If liked, 3 rashers of chopped streaky or back bacon can be used; just fry with the onion and garlic in step 1.

# Carrot & Ginger Soup

## Serves 4

4 slices bread, crusts removed
1 tsp yeast extract
2 tsp olive oil
1 onion, peeled and chopped
1 garlic clove, peeled and crushed
$^1/_2$ tsp ground ginger
450 g/1 lb carrots, peeled
and chopped
1 litre/1$^3/_4$ pints vegetable stock
2.5 cm/1 inch piece root ginger,
peeled and finely grated
salt and freshly ground
black pepper
1 tbsp lemon juice

## To garnish:

chives
lemon zest

Preheat the oven to 180°C/350°F/Gas Mark 4. Roughly chop the bread. Dissolve the yeast extract in 2 tablespoons warm water and mix with the bread.

Spread the bread cubes over a lightly oiled baking tray and bake for 20 minutes, turning halfway through. Remove from the oven and reserve.

Heat the oil in a large saucepan. Gently cook the onion and garlic for 3–4 minutes.

Stir in the ground ginger and cook for 1 minute to release the flavour.

Add the chopped carrots, then stir in the stock and the fresh ginger. Simmer gently for 15 minutes.

Remove from the heat and allow to cool a little. Blend until smooth, then season to taste with salt and pepper. Stir in the lemon juice. Garnish with the chives and lemon zest and serve immediately.

# Artichoke Soup with Croutons

## Serves 4

3 tbsp lemon juice
5 artichoke hearts
50 g/2 oz butter
1 leek, trimmed and sliced
4 large garlic cloves, peeled
and chopped
3 shallots, peeled and chopped
225 g/8 oz potatoes, peeled
and chopped
900 ml/1 1/2 pints vegetable stock
3–4 thyme sprigs
2 bay leaves
150 ml/1/4 pint milk
salt and freshly ground
black pepper
roughly chopped parsley, to garnish

## For the croutons:

2 large slices white bread
2–3 tbsp sunflower oil

Place the lemon juice in a small bowl of water. Peel off the leaves from around the artichokes thistle-like choke and remove. Cut away the thick part of the stem and cut the stem until it is about 5 cm/2 inches long. Thinly slice the hearts or chokes and place in the bowl of lemon water.

Melt the butter in a heavy-based saucepan, add the sliced hearts, leek, garlic, shallots and potatoes and cook for 5 minutes, or until the shallots are beginning to soften. Add the stock and the herbs, then bring to the boil. Reduce the heat, cover with a lid and simmer for 40–50 minutes until the vegetables are tender. Add a little extra stock if it is evaporating too quickly and reduce the heat a little more.

Leave the soup to cool, discard the bay leaves, then whizz in a food processor until smooth, adding the milk gradually. Return the soup to a clean saucepan and add seasoning to taste. Reheat gently, stirring occasionally, until hot.

While the soup is simmering, make the croutons by cutting the bread into small squares. Heat the oil in a heavy-based frying pan. When hot, add the bread and fry, stirring the bread and turning the squares over, for 2–3 minutes until golden and crisp. Drain on kitchen paper.

Ladle the soup into warmed bowls, garnish with parsley and croutons.

# Tomato & Basil Soup

### Serves 4

1.1 kg/ 2¹/₂ lb ripe tomatoes,
cut in half
2 garlic cloves
1 tsp olive oil
1 tbsp balsamic vinegar
1 tbsp dark brown sugar
1 tbsp tomato purée
300 ml/¹/₂ pint vegetable stock
6 tbsp natural yogurt
2 tbsp freshly chopped basil
salt and freshly ground
black pepper
small basil leaves,
to garnish

Preheat the oven to 200°C/400°F/Gas Mark 6. Evenly spread the tomatoes and unpeeled garlic in a single layer in a large roasting tin.

Mix the oil and vinegar together. Drizzle over the tomatoes and sprinkle with the dark brown sugar.

Roast the tomatoes in the preheated oven for 20 minutes until tender and lightly charred in places.

Remove from the oven and allow to cool slightly. When cool enough to handle, squeeze the softened flesh of the garlic from the papery skin. Place with the charred tomatoes in a nylon sieve over a saucepan.

Press the garlic and tomatoes through the sieve with the back of a wooden spoon.

When all the flesh has been sieved, add the tomato purée and vegetable stock to the pan. Heat gently, stirring occasionally.

In a small bowl, beat the yogurt and basil together and season to taste with salt and pepper. Stir the basil yogurt into the soup. Garnish with basil leaves and serve immediately.

# Mixed Veg Soup

### Serves 4

2 tbsp olive oil
2 medium onions, peeled
and chopped
2 garlic cloves, peeled and chopped
125 g/4 oz parsnips, peeled
and chopped
175 g/6 oz carrots, peeled
and chopped
175 g/6 oz potatoes, peeled
and chopped
2 celery stalks, trimmed
and chopped
1 large leek, trimmed and chopped
1 tbsp plain flour
900 ml/1 1/2 pints vegetable stock
2 bay leaves
salt and freshly ground
black pepper
parsley sprigs, to garnish
bread or toast, cut into cubes,
to serve

Heat the oil in a large saucepan, add the vegetables and fry for 5–8 minutes until the vegetables are beginning to soften, stirring frequently. Sprinkle in the flour, then cook for a further 3 minutes, stirring.

Add the stock with the bay leaves and bring to the boil. Reduce the heat, cover with a lid and simmer for 15–20 minutes until the vegetables are tender. Discard the bay leaves.

Leave to cool for at least 5 minutes, then whizz the soup in a food processor until smooth. Return to a clean saucepan and add the seasoning to taste. Reheat until hot, then ladle into warmed bowls, garnish with parsley and serve with bread or toast.

**Cook's Tip:** For a change, after making the soup and returning to the saucepan, add some cooked or drained canned beans, such as red kidney beans.

# Roasted Red Pepper, Tomato & Red Onion Soup

### Serves 4

fine spray of oil
2 large red peppers,
deseeded and roughly chopped
1 red onion, peeled and
roughly chopped
350 g/12 oz tomatoes, halved
1 small crusty French loaf
1 garlic clove, peeled
600 ml/1 pint vegetable stock
salt and freshly ground
black pepper
1 tsp Worcestershire sauce
4 tbsp fromage frais

Preheat the oven to 190°C/375°F/Gas Mark 5. Spray a large roasting tin with the oil and place the peppers and onion in the base. Cook in the oven for 10 minutes. Add the tomatoes and cook for a further 20 minutes or until the peppers are soft.

Cut the bread into 1 cm/½ inch slices. Cut the garlic clove in half and rub the cut edge of the garlic over the bread.

Place all the bread slices on a large baking tray, and bake in the preheated oven for 10 minutes, turning halfway through, until golden and crisp.

Remove the vegetables from the oven and allow to cool slightly, then blend in a food processor until smooth. Strain the vegetable mixture through a large nylon sieve into a saucepan, to remove the seeds and skin. Add the stock, season to taste with salt and pepper and stir to mix. Heat the soup gently until piping hot.

In a small bowl, beat together the Worcestershire sauce with the fromage frais.

Pour the soup into warmed bowls and swirl a spoonful of the fromage frais mixture into each bowl. Serve immediately with the garlic toasts.

# Vegetarian Minestrone

## Serves 4–6

2 tbsp olive oil
2 medium onions, peeled and
finely chopped
2–3 garlic cloves, peeled and
finely chopped
1 red pepper, finely chopped
1 green pepper, finely chopped
1 yellow pepper, finely chopped
1 leek, trimmed and chopped
1 celery stalk, trimmed and chopped
2 tbsp tomato purée
1.1 litres/2 pints vegetable stock
2 bay leaves
50 g/2 oz pasta, such as twists
or penne
4 medium tomatoes, cut into
small pieces
salt and freshly ground black pepper
bread slices, toasted, to serve

## To garnish:

fresh herbs, such as oregano or parsley
freshly grated Parmesan cheese

Heat the oil in a large saucepan, add the onions, garlic, peppers, leek and celery and cook for 5–8 minutes until the vegetables are beginning to soften.

Blend the tomato purée with a little stock, then add to the vegetables together with the remaining stock and bay leaves.

Add the pasta to the saucepan with the quartered tomatoes and seasoning to taste. Cook for 15–20 minutes until the vegetables and pasta are tender. Ladle into warmed bowls, garnish with herbs and grated Parmesan cheese and serve with toast.

**Cook's Tip:** Other vegetables can be used, depending on personal preference and availability. Try French beans, broccoli, carrots and shredded green cabbage.

# Swede, Turnip, Parsnip & Potato Soup

### Serves 4

2 large onions, peeled
25 g/1 oz butter
2 medium carrots, peeled and
roughly chopped
175 g/6 oz swede, peeled and
roughly chopped
125 g/4 oz turnip, peeled and
roughly chopped
125 g/4 oz parsnips, peeled and
roughly chopped
175 g/6 oz potatoes, peeled
1 litre/1³/₄ pints vegetable stock
¹/₂ tsp freshly grated nutmeg
salt and freshly ground
black pepper
4 tbsp vegetable oil, for frying
125 ml/4 fl oz double cream
warm crusty bread, to serve

Finely chop 1 onion. Melt the butter in a large saucepan and add the onion, carrots, swede, turnips, parsnips and potatoes. Cover with a lid and cook gently for about 10 minutes, without colouring. Stir occasionally during this time.

Add the stock and season to taste with the nutmeg, salt and pepper. Cover and bring to the boil, then reduce the heat and simmer gently for 15–20 minutes until the vegetables are tender. Remove from the heat and leave to cool for 30 minutes.

Heat the oil in a large, heavy-based frying pan. Add the remaining onions, sliced, and cook over a medium heat for about 2–3 minutes, stirring frequently, until golden brown. Remove the onions with a slotted spoon and drain well on absorbent kitchen paper. As they cool, they will turn crispy.

Pour the cooled soup into a food processor or blender and process to form a smooth purée. Return to the cleaned pan, adjust the seasoning, then stir in the cream. Gently reheat and top with the crispy onions. Serve immediately with chunks of bread.

# Cream of Aubergine Soup

### Serves 4

450 g/1 lb aubergine
2 medium onions
4 garlic cloves
450 g/1 lb large tomatoes
3 tbsp olive oil
1 tsp ground coriander
$^1/_2$ tsp ground cumin
$^1/_2$ tsp turmeric
900 ml/1$^1/_2$ pints vegetable stock
salt and freshly ground
black pepper
175 g/6 oz feta cheese
mint leaves, to garnish

Preheat the oven to 200°C/400°F/Gas Mark 6, 15 minutes before cooking. Cut the aubergines in half lengthways and place in a roasting tin. Cut the tomatoes in half and place in the roasting tin. Peel the onions and garlic and chop roughly, then scatter over the aubergines and tomatoes.

Blend the oil with the spices, then drizzle over the vegetables and stir until coated in the spicy oil. Roast in the oven for 40–45 minutes until the aubergines and onions are tender, stirring occasionally during roasting. Remove from the oven and leave to cool.

When cool enough to handle, scoop out the aubergine flesh and place in a food processor. Discard the tomato skin and place the flesh in the processor together with the onions and garlic. Add 300 ml/$^1/_2$ pint of the stock and blend until smooth, adding more stock as necessary.

Pour the soup into a saucepan together with any remaining stock. Season to taste and crumble in about two thirds of the feta. Heat gently until hot, then ladle into warmed bowls and top with the remaining feta, then garnish with mint leaves.

**Cook's Tip:** Providing that the aubergines are young, there is no need to sprinkle them with salt before using.

# Cream of Spinach Soup

## Serves 4

1 large onion, peeled and chopped
5 large, plump garlic cloves,
peeled and chopped
2 medium potatoes, peeled
and chopped
750 ml/1¼ pints cold water
1 tsp salt
450 g/1 lb spinach, washed and
large stems removed
50 g/2 oz butter
3 tbsp flour
750 ml/1¼ pints milk
½ tsp freshly grated nutmeg,
or to taste
freshly ground black pepper
6–8 tbsp crème fraîche or
sour cream
warm focaccia bread, to serve

Place the onion, garlic and potatoes in a large saucepan and cover with the cold water. Add half the salt and bring to the boil. Cover with a lid and simmer for 15–20 minutes until the potatoes are tender. Remove from the heat and add the spinach. Cover and set aside for 10 minutes.

Slowly melt the butter in another saucepan, add the flour and cook over a low heat for about 2 minutes. Remove the saucepan from the heat and add the milk, a little at a time, stirring continuously. Return to the heat and cook, stirring continuously, for 5–8 minutes until the sauce is smooth and slightly thickened. Add the freshly grated nutmeg to taste.

Blend the cooled potato and spinach mixture to a smooth purée in a food processor or blender, then return to the saucepan and gradually stir in the white sauce. Season to taste with salt and pepper and gently reheat, taking care not to allow the soup to boil. Ladle into soup bowls and top with spoonfuls of crème fraîche or sour cream. Serve immediately with warm focaccia bread.

# Apple ❧ Leek Soup

## Serves 4

25 g/1 oz butter
350 g/12 oz leeks, trimmed
and sliced
225 g/8 oz potatoes, peeled
and chopped
225 g/8 oz Bramley apples, peeled,
cored and chopped
900 ml/1½ pints vegetable stock
3 thyme sprigs, plus extra to garnish
salt and freshly ground
black pepper
150 ml/¼ pint milk

Heat the butter in a large saucepan and, when melted, add the leeks, potatoes and apples and cook for 5 minutes, or until they are coated in the butter.

Pour in the stock and bring to the boil. Reduce the heat, add the thyme, cover with a lid and simmer for 15–20 minutes until the vegetables are well cooked and tender. Remove from the heat and leave to cool for 5 minutes.

When cool, whizz the soup in a food processor until smooth, then return to a clean saucepan. Add seasoning to taste and stir in the milk. Reheat gently, then serve in warmed bowls, garnished with thyme sprigs.

Cook's Tip: When using apples in cooking, it is advisable to use an apple specifically grown for cooking. Bramley apples are the best in the UK.

# Curried Parsnip Soup

### Serves 4

1 tsp cumin seeds
2 tsp coriander seeds
1 tsp oil
1 onion, peeled and chopped
1 garlic clove, peeled
and crushed
$^1/_2$ tsp turmeric
$^1/_4$ tsp chilli powder
1 cinnamon stick
450 g/1 lb parsnips, peeled
and chopped
1 litre/1$^3/_4$ pint vegetable stock
salt and freshly ground
black pepper
fresh coriander leaves,
to garnish
2–3 tbsp natural yogurt,
to serve

In a small frying pan, dry-fry the cumin and coriander seeds over a moderately high heat for 1–2 minutes. Shake the pan during cooking until the seeds are lightly toasted.

Reserve until cooled. Grind the toasted seeds in a pestle and mortar.

Heat the oil in a saucepan. Cook the onion until softened and starting to turn golden.

Add the garlic, turmeric, chilli powder and cinnamon stick to the pan. Continue to cook for a further minute.

Add the parsnips and stir well. Pour in the stock and bring to the boil. Cover with a lid and simmer for 15 minutes, or until the parsnips are cooked.

Allow the soup to cool. Once cooled, remove the cinnamon stick and discard.

Blend the soup in a food processor until very smooth.

Transfer to a saucepan and reheat gently. Season to taste with salt and pepper. Garnish with fresh coriander and serve immediately with the yogurt.

# Cream of Mushroom Soup

## Serves 4

350 g/12 oz closed cup
mushrooms, sliced
1 medium onion, peeled
and chopped
1 celery stalk, trimmed
and chopped
475 ml/¾ pint vegetable stock
50 g/2 oz butter
50 g/2 oz plain flour
350ml/12 fl oz milk
salt and freshly ground black or
white pepper
4 tbsp single cream
1 tbsp freshly chopped parsley or
chervil, to garnish
brown bread, to serve

Place the mushrooms, onion and celery in a large saucepan with the stock and bring to the boil. Reduce the heat, cover with a lid and simmer for 30 minutes, or until the mushrooms are very tender. Leave to cool.

When the vegetables have cooled slightly, whizz in a food processor to form a purée. Reserve.

Melt the butter in a clean saucepan, then stir in the flour. Cook over a medium heat for 3 minutes, stirring. Remove from the heat and gradually stir in the milk then the mushroom purée and cook, stirring, until the mixture thickens.

Add seasoning to taste and continue to heat until hot. Stir in the cream and continue to heat, stirring, for 2–3 minutes. Garnish with the chopped herbs and serve with brown bread.

**Cook's Tip:** When preparing mushrooms, do not wash but wipe with kitchen paper, as the mushrooms are porous and their flavour is lost if they are washed.

# Nettle Soup

## Serves 4

450 g/1 lb nettle leaves
2 tbsp olive oil
2 medium onions, peeled and
finely chopped
2–3 garlic cloves, peeled and
finely chopped
1 medium leek, trimmed and sliced
300 g/11 oz potatoes, peeled
and chopped
1 tbsp plain flour
4 tbsp orange juice
1 bouquet garni
900 ml/1½ pints vegetable stock
salt and freshly ground black pepper
150 ml/¼ pint single cream or
crème fraîche, plus extra
to garnish
fresh herbs or nettle flowers,
to garnish

Wearing rubber gloves, pick over the nettle leaves, discarding any stalks, damaged or very tired leaves, then wash thoroughly and reserve.

Heat the oil in a large saucepan over a medium heat, add the onions, garlic, leek and potatoes and stir lightly until they are coated in the oil. Cook for 8–10 minutes until they are beginning to soften. Sprinkle in the flour and cook for 1–2 minutes.

Add the nettle leaves and orange juice and cook for a further 5 minutes, or until the leaves are wilting. Add the bouquet garni and stock. Bring to the boil, reduce the heat, cover with a lid and simmer for 20 minutes, or until the vegetables are completely tender.

Remove the pan from the heat and discard the bouquet garni. Leave to cool for 5 minutes, then whizz in a food processor until smooth. Return the soup to a clean saucepan, add seasoning to taste, then stir in the cream or crème fraîche and reheat for 3–4 minutes. Ladle into warmed soup bowls, garnish with extra cream or crème fraîche and herbs or nettle flowers and serve.

**Cook's Tip:** Nettles are best eaten when young and before they flower in late May. Pick the tips and be sure to wash them thoroughly to remove any unwanted bugs.

# Index